I0764888

THE PENINSULA

D. C. Buell

THE ARMY IN THE CIVIL WAR

VOLUME III.

THE PENINSULA—McCLELLAN'S CAMPAIGN OF 1862

BY

ALEXANDER S. WEBB, LL.D.

PRESIDENT OF THE COLLEGE OF THE CITY OF NEW YORK; ASSISTANT CHIEF OF ARTILLERY, ARMY OF THE POTOMAC; INSPECTOR-GENERAL, FIFTH ARMY CORPS; GENERAL COMMANDING SECOND DIVISION, SECOND CORPS; MAJOR-GENERAL ASSIGNED, AND CHIEF OF STAFF, ARMY OF THE POTOMAC.

SUBSCRIPTION EDITION

CHARLES SCRIBNER'S SONS

NEW YORK

TROW'S
PRINTING AND BOOKBINDING COMPANY,
NEW YORK.

THE ARMY IN THE CIVIL WAR
THE PENINSULA - McCLELLAN'S CAMPAIGN OF 1862
VOLUME III.

By Alexander S. Webb LL.D.

As Published in 1885

Trade Paperback ISBN: 1-58218-529-8
Hardcover ISBN: 1-58218-545-X
eBook ISBN: 1-58218-561-1

Digital Scanning and Publishing is a leader in the electronic republication of historical books and documents. We publish many of our titles as eBooks, as well as traditional hardcover and trade paper editions. DSI is committed to bringing many traditional and little known books back to life, retaining the look and feel of the original work.

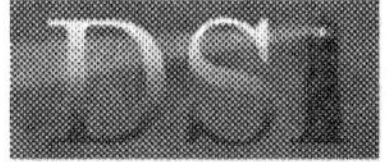

First DSI Printing: October 2001

Published by DIGITAL SCANNING, INC.
Scituate, MA 02066
www.digitalscanning.com

PREFACE.

To be of any practical use, all history, and particularly military history, must be gradually sifted and reduced to small compass. To carry out this idea, the publishers have asked the writer to prepare for them, in a condensed form, that part of the History of the War of the Rebellion which includes the operations of the Army of the Potomac from the assumption of the command of that army by General McClellan, in July, 1861, to its arrival at Harrison's Landing, in July, 1862.

So much has been written on this subject that it would not at first appear to be a difficult matter to condense the various accounts; but to the writer's task has been added the special work required in comparing and collating for careful investigation the *new material* gathered by the War Department, and now for the first time made the basis of a history of that period. The results of that labor he presents in these pages.

An actor himself in everything here treated of, he has in a large measure been guided in his research by his memory of scenes never to be effaced, but not by the false impressions of those days, with which, on most occasions, he was heartily in accord.

In speaking of the "President of the United States and his advisers," he must not be understood as recalling or changing at any time his constant and repeated expressions of admiration, affection and regard for the President himself. He appeals to the closing chapter, reviewing the whole work of the army during the twelve months covered by this volume, to prove that he is as loyal to that noble man's memory as ever he was to him in person, and is but doing the work of an honest historian in recording the sad tale of the want of unity, the want of confidence, the want of co-operation between the Administration and the General commanding the army.

In this work we cannot give *in extenso* the most important of the better-known documents, so often printed by the writers on both sides of the questions which arose between General McClellan and the Administration, and omit every one not absolutely necessary to a proper understanding of the narrative. We hope, however, that the attention of thinking men will be attracted to a more thorough investigation of the questions not yet settled, and that this work will serve as an aid to any one who desires to seek what is the vital lesson to be derived from our failure on the Peninsula.

We have been unable to do justice to many of our most gallant officers or to their commands, by giving in full the history of their achievements during this campaign. We have been limited in the space assigned to this narrative, and we have been forced to choose between repeating the well-known accounts of various battles and giving from new data the proof of the restless and daring activity of the Rebels who fought us. We have chosen the latter course, believing that there is a public demand for information of this kind. Our sketch of the campaign will, we hope, serve as a reliable introduction to a larger volume.

We are under especial obligations to Secretary of War Lincoln, to Secretary of the Navy Hunt, to Colonel Robert N. Scott, of the Bureau of Archives in the War Department, to Generals Wright, Meigs, Barnes, Humphreys, Keyes, and others, for their continued kindness in furnishing maps and documents, during the four months in which we have been engaged in the preparation of this volume.

NEW YORK CITY,
November, 1881.

CONTENTS.

CHAPTER VIII.

CHAPTER IX.

APPENDIX A.

APPENDIX B.

LIST OF MAPS.

THE PENINSULA.

CHAPTER I.

GENERAL McCLELLAN AND THE ARMY OF THE POTOMAC.

WHEN the Union troops returned to Washington from the disastrous field of Manassas, or the better known Bull Run, the usual results of a defeat, where the forces engaged have been raw levies led by untried and unskilled commanders, were presented to the general Government. The capital of the nation was almost within the lines of the rebellious territory. All that was most demoralized or least apt to present either a truthful or fair account of the incidents of the few past days swarmed in the streets of Washington, and through the medium of a sensitive press spread alarm on every side. From such a presentation of the situation in front, it was not to be expected that the Government, surrounded by every evidence of the complete discomfiture of its main army, would be found either ready to view the reverses calmly or to act with the boldness and promptitude which the sudden events then demanded. Centreville, the key-point, or point of safety, twenty miles in advance of Washington, was given up; the reserves, under Colonel Miles, were allowed to leave it; and the whole force of the

III.—1

nation was immediately called into action to solve the great problem—how to regain the abandoned position and finally compel the submission of the enemy.

The rebels, at first no wiser than ourselves, were there taught that, by a little attention to our general tardiness or want of prompt decision in cases of emergency, they might hold their interior lines for an indefinite period. Men on the defensive are receptive scholars, and we found that our adversaries had learned this great lesson still more perfectly after our bitter experience in the Peninsula campaign.

On July 21st the streets of Washington were crowded with stragglers from the Army of the Potomac. On July 22d, General George B. McClellan was relieved from command of the Army of the West, and that command was given to General W. S. Rosecrans. On July 27th, General McClellan, by order of President Lincoln, assumed control of the lately defeated troops in the vicinity of the capital.

Who was this new general selected to produce order and organize our armies?

George Brinton McClellan was born in Philadelphia, December 3, 1826. He entered the Military Academy in June, 1842, and graduated in June, 1846. After serving under Captain A. J. Smith and Lieutenant Gustavus W. Smith, with the new engineer company of sappers and miners at West Point, he sailed for the army in Mexico in September, 1846, and served with especial distinction until the army under General Scott entered the capital, on September 14, 1847. For distinguished services and personal gallantry he was breveted first lieutenant and captain, to date from the day of the capture of that city. He served at West Point with the Engineer Company; with Captain Randolph B. Marcy, Fifth Infantry, in making the explorations of the country embraced within the basin of the upper Red River; on the staff of General Persifor F. Smith, in Texas, as Chief Engineer; under Governor Isaac I. Stevens, of Washington Territory, examining the lines of the forty-seventh and forty-ninth parallels of north latitude, and determining a railroad route from the head waters of the Mississippi to Puget Sound; was detailed to select a coaling-station in the West Indies; and employed on duties in Washington connected with the Pacific Railroad surveys. In all these various positions he exhibited the largest capacity and the most commendable zeal. As a reward and as an exhibit of the special favor in which he was held by the United States Government, he was appointed one of the Military Commission to Europe to observe the operations in the Crimea. With him were associated General Delafield and Major Mordecai, then majors in the regular army.

At that time he was in his twenty-ninth year, and was one of the youngest captains in the United States Army. Returning from this duty, after hard mental labor, and after gaining a valuable experience as an officer, he served in various stations until 1857, when he resigned his commission and accepted the appointment of Chief Engineer of the Illinois Central Railroad, of which corporation he was made Vice-President in a very short period. In 1860 he was chosen President of the Ohio & Mississippi Railroad, and resided in Cincinnati until the war of the rebellion.

When the rebels had taken Sumter, and the North was turning to the graduates of the military academy for assistance and direction in the organization of the new troops to be ordered into the field, Governor William Denison, of Ohio, naturally sought the advice and counsel of George B. McClellan, and finally appointed him Major-General of the "Militia Volunteers" of that State. His friends realized that he had a heavy task before him, but his large experience and general military education rendered him equal to its requirements, and he readily organized, equipped, and put in the field the Army of the Department of the Ohio. As the result of his operations in Western Virginia the Government of the United States received from that army the glad intelligence of the rout of Garnett and Pegram, on July 12 and 13, 1861. It was, therefore, but natural that he should have been summoned to Washington to recreate the army which was destined to defend the capital for the next three years.

From July 27th to October 31st, General McClellan remained in command of the Army of the Potomac only, until, on November 1st, he assumed control of the armies of the United States in accordance with General Order No. 94. His own order of that date is noteworthy, as coming from so young an officer on assuming so vast a responsibility. His subsequent orders to General Buell, in charge of the Department of the Ohio, and General Halleck, in charge of that of the Missouri, together with his letters to General Sherman, commanding at Port Royal, and to General Butler in the Southwest, show the vigor of thought and the grasp of the man who had been called to the prosecution of a war which extended over half the continent. He perfected a grand scheme, in which all the armies were to bear their part, and in which the Army of the Potomac had only its subordinate movements assigned to it.

General McClellan became the Commander-in-Chief of the forces of the United States through the expressed will of the people and with the approval of the veteran General Scott. No higher compliment could have been paid the new commander than that contained in the message of President Lincoln, in December, 1861, when he says, that "the retiring chief expressed his judgment in favor of General McClellan for the position, and in this the nation seemed to give an unanimous concurrence."

Such was the man who was to command the Army of the Potomac in its campaign against Richmond. No one had then the right to complain or to protest against his appointment. He was at that date our most successful general. He accepted the full responsibility devolved upon him, and the nation has much to thank him for. It was he who organized, equipped, and trained, with skill, that grand body of troops which for four long years "confronted the strongest, best appointed, and most confident army in the South."*

Upon reaching Washington, on July 27, 1861, the General found the forces in and around the city numbering about fifty thousand infantry, less than one thousand cavalry, and six hundred and fifty artillerymen, with nine imperfect field-batteries of thirty pieces and four hundred horses. No more faithful picture of the situation there could be presented than is to be found in the General's own report, as follows:

"On the Virginia bank of the Potomac the brigade organization of General McDowell still existed, and the troops were stationed at and in rear of Forts Corcoran, Arlington, and Fort Albany, at Fort Runyon, Roach's Mills, Cole's Mills, and in the vicinity of Fort Ellsworth, with a detachment at the Theological Seminary, near Alexandria. These were no troops south of Hunting Creek, and many of the regiments were encamped on the low grounds bordering the Potomac—seldom in the best positions for defence, and entirely inadequate in numbers and condition to defend the long line from Fort Corcoran to Alexandria. On the Mary-

* Grant to Washburne, December 23, 1864.

land side of the river, upon the heights overlooking the Chain Bridge, two regiments were stationed, whose commanders were independent of each other. There were no troops on the important Tenallytown road, or on the roads entering the city from the south. The camps were located without regard to purposes of defence or instruction; the roads were not picketed, and there was no attempt at an organization into brigades.

"In no quarter were the dispositions for defence such as to offer a vigorous resistance to a respectable body of the enemy, either in the positions or numbers of the troops, or the number and character of the defensive works. Earthworks, in the nature of *têtes-de-pont* looked upon the approaches to the Georgetown aqueduct and ferry, the Long Bridge, and Alexandria, by the Little River Turnpike, and some simple defensive arrangements were made at the Chain Bridge. With the latter exception, not a single defensive work had been constructed on the Maryland side. There was nothing to prevent the enemy from shelling the city from the opposite heights, which were within easy range, and which could have been occupied by a hostile column almost without resistance. Many soldiers had deserted, and the streets of Washington were crowded with straggling officers and men, absent from their stations without authority, whose behavior indicated the general want of discipline and organization."

General McClellan immediately appointed his general staff, and the work of receiving, organizing, and preparing for the field an enormous army was forthwith undertaken. On October 27, 1861, he officially reported to the Secretary of War that on that date there were present *for duty* 147,695 men, with an aggregate strength of 168,318. Of this number, 4,268 cavalry were completely unarmed, 3,163 partially armed, 5,979 infantry unequipped—making 13,410 unfit for the field, but leaving an effective force of 134,285. He states that he had 76,285 men disposable for an advance, but had but two hundred and twenty-eight artillery pieces ready for the field, and required one hundred and twelve more. This seems to have been a rapid increase for the army in ninety days, being an addition of 40,000 men per month.*

Proceeding to its efficient organization, the General formed the new levies of infantry, upon their arrival in Washington, into provisional brigades, and stationed them in the suburbs of the city to be perfected by instruction and discipline. Brigadier-General F. J. Porter was at first assigned to the charge of these brigades. He was followed by Brigadier-General A. E. Burnside, who, in turn, was soon after relieved by Brigadier-General Silas Casey, who continued in charge of the constantly arriving regiments until the Army embarked for the Peninsula in March, 1862. The new artillery troops reported to Brigadier-General William F. Barry,

* The following abstract from the consolidated monthly returns of the Army of the Potomac shows its strength, from November 30, 1861, to the time it took the field on the Peninsula, inclusive of troops in the Shenandoah, on the Potomac, and at posts in the vicinity of Washington:

Date of Returns.	PRESENT FOR DUTY.		Aggregate present and absent.	PIECES OF ARTILLERY.		
	Officers.	Men.		Heavy.	Field.	Mountain
November 30, 1861	6,867	155,870	198,238	133	248	2
December 31, 1861	7,653	175,854	219,781	221	293	—
January 31, 1862	7,842	174,831	222,227	92	381	2
February 28, 1862	7,862	177,556	222,018	69	465	1
March 31, 1862	7,760	171,602	214,983	242	440	6

Records Adjutant-General's Office.

the Chief of Artillery, and the cavalry to Brigadier-General George Stoneman, Chief of Cavalry.

By the opening of the spring of 1862 the expectations of General McClellan appear to have been realized in the creation of as noble a body of men as could have been raised, under similar circumstances, the world over. Exclusive of detachments necessary to garrison the defences of Washington and Alexandria, to retain Manassas and Warrenton, to watch the Valley of the Shenandoah, and guard the Maryland shore of the Potomac, both above and below the capital, which together mustered fifty-five thousand strong, the army proper, intended by its commander to act as a solid body for field operations, represented a force, on the rolls, of 158,000 men. At the close of this volume is inserted a roster showing its final composition and organization, to which the interested reader may wish to refer. From an examination of the tables there given, we may deduce much that would seem to secure to the General-in-Chief, for his labors, the respect and admiration of his countrymen. At the same time, to have been enabled to establish a force of such proportions and efficiency within a few months, he must necessarily have received from the general Government, from the governors of the several States, and from the various bureaus and offices under the War Department, the most cordial and largest assistance. Without that support, and without almost superhuman efforts on their part, such an army could never have been created.

It was an army, furthermore, which was thoroughly representative; an army of volunteers, composing, with the armies elsewhere in the field, the nation's *posse comitatus*. The troops immediately under the leadership of General McClellan, in March, 1862—this Army of the Potomac—were drawn, naturally, from the Eastern and Atlantic States of the Union, as the armies operating along the lines of the Tennessee and Mississippi were recruited, in the main, from the Central States and the great Northwest. The New England States contributed a quota of some thirty-five regiments; New York, seventy; New Jersey, ten; Pennsylvania, sixty; Delaware, one; Maryland, nine (posted chiefly along the Potomac); while Ohio, Illinois, Indiana, Wisconsin, and Minnesota were also in line with from one to three thousand men each. The little corps of regulars, mustering in August, 1861, only a thousand strong, had been increased by April 30, 1862, to a respectable and highly effective brigade of 4,600, rank and file, under Brigadier-General George Sykes, then Major of the Third Infantry. Irrespective of the latter, the mass of the army was composed of intelligent voters, coming from every walk in life. It represented the bone and sinew of the land, its truest homes and best industries, its humblest, its toiling, its prosperous, and its educated classes alike. They were men, the vast majority of them, who thoroughly understood the merits of the struggle, who appreciated the value of the principle at stake, who believed they were right, and were ready to support their convictions and their Government with their blood. It was, indeed, a people's cause and a people's war. Bull Run had neither dispirited nor overawed them. That defeat had served only to bring into clearer light the magnitude and desperate character of the work in hand, and they girded their loins for the emergency. They were, in a word, as they have been and always must be described, an organized collection of citizen-soldiers, who did not despair of the Union, and only prayed that they might be ably led against the enemy, that their services and sacrifices might contribute decisively to success.

CHAPTER II.

CAMPAIGN PLANS.

NECESSARILY, soon after assuming his duties as Commander-in-Chief, General McClellan turned his attention to the entire field of operations, treating the Army of the Potomac as only one, although the most important of the several armies under his control. Already, as Department Commander, he had prepared for the President, at the latter's request, a memorandum setting forth his views as to the proper method of suppressing the rebellion, which views he still retained, and upon which, it is generally claimed by his friends, the subsequent successful campaigns were practically based. He proposed to strike at two centres, East and West—Richmond and Nashville—moving thus into the heart of secession; while, at the same time, expeditionary forces were to assail the principal points on the coast, and on and beyond the Mississippi. War all along the line was his purpose. While he himself marched down into Virginia, General Buell, in Eastern Kentucky, was to secure that State, relieve Eastern Tennessee, and then point to Nashville; General Halleck was to look after the troublesome State of Missouri, and Western Kentucky, and Tennessee; General Burnside was to occupy the coast of North Carolina; General T. W. Sherman was to seize Savannah, but chiefly to prepare to regain Charleston; for by the capture of that city, "the greatest moral effect would be produced," as it was the birthplace of the rebellion, and "the centre of the boasted power and courage of the rebels;" and lastly, General Butler was to attempt the recovery of New Orleans, by which, the eventual control of the Mississippi could be more easily established.

That this extensive plan might work effectually, General McClellan aimed to deliver the meditated blows, or the principal ones, simultaneously. The responsibility, accordingly, devolved upon him to have everything ready everywhere at the proper moment. This alone would have been a great task, especially as he claims that no general plan existed before his assumption of the chief command, and that he was wholly ignorant of the "utter disorganization and want of preparation" that pervaded the Western armies. "The labor of creation and organization had to be performed there" as well as in the East, says the General; and by January 1, 1862, the forward movement was still delayed. Several months thus passed devoted to preparation, and the country for the most part, understanding that the inaction was necessary, quietly awaited the compensating results that were expected to follow when active movements should begin.

But the trouble was that the delay was protracted too long, even for a patient people. The fall of 1861 passed, and the rebels were as strong as ever and more defiant. The following winter also promised to be one of stagnation, especially for the Army of the Potomac, and soon toward the close of 1861, and in the beginning of 1862, much curiosity and uneasiness was betrayed respecting the intentions of the new and then popular Commander-in-Chief. The latter, however, was clearly determined not to be hurried. As late as February 3, 1862, he wrote to the President, "I have ever regarded our true policy as being that of fully preparing ourselves, and then seeking for the most decisive results;" and it was not until a short time before that date, that he disclosed his own plan of campaign in Virginia to the Government authorities. His inaction he reported to be unavoidable. Preparations for the execution of the general plan—the simultaneous movement—were incomplete. He had hoped that everything would have been ready to take advantage of the good weather in the previous December, but it was not. His own army even, he declared, was not yet in condition to take the field. "We are still delayed," he told the President, in his February letter, and, furthermore, gave no hint as to the time when he should be completely ready.

How this unfortunate situation might have been avoided—what General McClellan ought to have done during those six months his army remained around Washington—is a speculative question which we do not feel called upon to consider. It will be enough to discuss the plan for action which he finally did propose, and to follow out his movements in the field when actually undertaken. That the delay, however satisfactory or unsatisfactory his own explanation and defence of it may be regarded, worked to his disadvantage and paved the way for future distrust of his generalship, is certain. He drew too heavily upon the faith of the public. By March 1st the nation had incurred a debt of $600,000,000 for the war; while the results were far from commensurate with such a cost. Dissatisfaction arose, especially at Washington, in Government circles, and in Congress. Criticisms were freely indulged in. The General, in addition, kept his councils to himself, consulted with but one or two favorite officers, and seemed to hold close relations with men not in political sympathy with the Administration. All this gave umbrage in high places; and it became the more incumbent upon him to act, to act speedily, energetically, and successfully, if he hoped to retain the confidence of the powers to which he was amenable, or entitle himself to the obligations of a grateful people.

At length General McClellan was compelled to divulge his plans and move forward; and this brings us to some important points in the history of the campaign.

Among those who deeply felt the necessity of renewing the advance upon the enemy, was President Lincoln. An immense and oppressive responsibility rested upon his shoulders. He was constantly anxious both in success and defeat; and extremely anxious now, at the close of the year 1861. The situation was anything but satisfactory. In October previous, the disastrous affair of Ball's Bluff had occurred, in which Colonel Baker, lately of the Senate, lost his life. The rebels, also, had blocked the navigation of the Potomac by planting batteries on the Virginia side twenty or thirty miles down the river; and their flag floated insultingly, from their advanced works on Munson's Hill, in sight of Washington. These untoward circumstances, and the inactivity of McClellan, seemed to have prompted the President, as early as December 1st, to propose informally to the General, a plan of attack upon the enemy—his idea being that a column of 50,000 men should menace and hold the rebels at their Centreville position, while 50,000 more—part going by the Potomac, and part by land—should move to Occoquan Creek below, and place themselves nearer to Richmond than the main body of the enemy were at Centreville. This is interesting, not only as being the first plan, so far as the writer can discover from the records, suggested for the campaign, but as emanating from Mr. Lincoln himself, who made no pretensions to military knowledge; thus disclosing his intense desire that something should be done.

Up to this time, General McClellan had given no intimation of his own plans, other than the general assertion, made in the latter part of October, that "the crushing defeat of the rebel army at Manassas," was the great object to be accomplished; and that the advance upon it "should not be postponed beyond November 25th." On December 10th, however, he wrote a confidential note to the President, apparently in answer to the latter's proposal, in which he impliedly disapproved of it, by stating that he believed the enemy's force to be equal to his own; and then added, "I have now my mind actually turned toward *another plan of campaign* that I do not think at all anticipated by the enemy, nor by many of our own people."* This is the first hint we have that any plan was taking shape in the General's mind; and the first that foreshadowed the final move to the Peninsula.

It will be observed, that here was the possibility of a serious conflict of opinion. In case the President and the General matured plans diametrically opposed to each other, which was to be followed? What is our highest military authority? According to the Constitution, it is the President, Commander-in-Chief of all the land and naval forces of the United States. But if the President disclaims all military ability, as Mr. Lincoln did, it still becomes a question how far he should defer the conduct of a war to his generals commanding in the field. In the closing chapter of this work certain precedents are adduced upon this point, showing the position assumed by our Presidents during the War of 1812 and the Mexican War. They asserted their right to disapprove and interfere, and the propriety of their interference seemed to be justified. There never was any question in President Lincoln's case, as to his right to order and direct; but the dilemma lay here—whose plans and ad-

* See Appendix to Raymond's Life of Lincoln for this note and the President's plan referred to.

vice should he follow where it was necessary for him to approve and decide, where he did not or would not trust his own judgment? Should he lean implicitly on the general actually in command of the armies, placed there by virtue of his presumed fitness for the position, or upon other selected advisers? We are bold to say that it was doubt and hesitation upon this point, that occasioned many of the blunders of the campaign. Instead of one mind, there were many minds influencing the management of military affairs.

To one source of this influence, beyond the members of the President's Cabinet, who were by right his advisers, we must revert. This was the Joint Committee of Congress, appointed in December, 1861, to inquire into the conduct of the war. Its members were Hons. Benjamin F. Wade, of Ohio, Zachariah Chandler, of Michigan, and Andrew Johnson, of Tennessee, from the Senate; and Hons. Daniel W. Gooch, of Massachusetts, John Covode, of Pennsylvania, George W. Julian, of Indiana, and Moses F. Odell, of New York, from the House of Representatives. Organizing December 20th, with Senator Wade as chairman, it proceeded to summon many of the general officers of the army to obtain their views as to its efficiency, and the best lines of advance upon the enemy. It was a strong representative committee, and not only held consultations with the President and the new Secretary of War, Hon. Edwin M. Stanton, but also with the President and his entire Cabinet. No record of these interviews appears to have been preserved; but no one can doubt their effect upon the Administration in influencing its action. Executive, Cabinet and Committee, were in earnest in their wish to prosecute the war to a speedy and successful termination.

In common with the President and the country at large, this Committee was entirely dissatisfied with the prolonged inactivity of the Army of the Potomac. The members were especially mortified and indignant that the rebels should have been suffered to blockade the Potomac River so long, preventing free access by water to the capital of the nation, and thereby seriously affecting our delicate relations abroad. They demanded from the Secretary of War that the blockade should be raised—the chairman, on one occasion, using "pretty strong and emphatic language" on the subject in the presence of both the Secretary and General McClellan; and in their report the Committee lay the blame upon the General, who, in his report, holds the navy accountable. Again, the Committee examined many officers on the subject of organizing the army into corps; and finding great unanimity as to the necessity of such organization, pressed the matter upon the attention of the President more than once. Their last consultation with him on this subject occurred on March 5th, when he promised to take the matter "into earnest and serious consideration." Three days later, on the 8th, he promulgated an order dividing the army into four army corps, to the command of which Generals McDowell, Sumner, Heintzelman, and Keyes were assigned. The order was contrary to the wishes of McClellan, who proposed to defer the organization until after active operations had opened. The Committee, furthermore, obtained opinions from officers as to the best line of attack for the army to follow; and seemed to have become impressed with the superior advantages of a direct advance upon Centreville. That its preferences were known to the President, can hardly be questioned. Indeed, without a particular examination of the proceedings of this important Committee and a proper estimate of its influence, the action of Mr. Lincoln and his Cabinet, in certain matters affecting this campaign, cannot be fully understood. That body must be counted among the President's most influential advisers. It was a power during the war.

Returning to the plan of the campaign, we find that Mr. Lincoln, who on December 1st had suggested operating against the enemy in front and flank, took up the matter again early in January following, by seeking the opinions of a few of the more prominent generals in the army. General McClellan had had the misfortune of falling ill about the middle of December, and was confined to his house for nearly a month. Mr. Lincoln, more than ever exercised and worried over the delays, called in Generals McDowell and Franklin, and in a confidential interview inquired as to the possibility of soon commencing active operations with the Army of the Potomac. The President stated that "if something was not soon done, the bottom would be out of the whole affair." * A day or two later these officers, who had consulted with Quartermaster-General Meigs and others, reported, that of the two lines of attack considered—one direct upon the enemy, the other by moving the army to another base down the Chesapeake—they advised the former, which could be undertaken in three weeks.† General McClellan, recovering from his illness, and finding that "excessive anxiety for an immediate movement of the Army of the Potomac had taken possession of the minds of the Administration," finally unfolded his plan of operations to the President, which contemplated an attack upon Richmond by the lower Chesapeake. He was not in favor of a direct attack upon

* General McDowell's memorandum in Swinton's "Army of the Potomac."

† General Franklin, it seems, favoured a movement by way of the *York River,* and so testified before the Committee on the Conduct of the War; but according to General McDowell's statements (in Swinton) he deffered his plan in favour of a direct attack on the enemy as the most feasible *at that time,* namely, in January, and because of the President's wish for *immediate* action.

the enemy at Centreville. But the President had now become confirmed in his preference for the latter plan by the opinions of McDowell, Franklin and Meigs; and undoubtedly, as stated above, by the known preferences of the Committee on the Conduct of the War. We thus find the two leaders upon whom the eyes of the nation were then fixed—Mr. Lincoln and General McClellan—at issue with each other at a most critical moment.

It has been, and probably always will be one of the standing questions of dispute in this campaign, whose plan was the soundest, the President's or the General's? The President, certainly, was so far convinced of the advisability of adopting his own, or, as it may be called, the Administration plan, that he formally disapproved of McClellan's, and in a *special* war order, "No. 1," dated January 31st, directed that the Army of the Potomac, "after providing safely for the defence of Washington," should move forward, on or before February 22d, and seize and occupy a point upon the railroad southwest of Manassas Junction. The first effect of this, would be the withdrawal of the enemy from their position in front of the capital. Four days before—January 27th—the President had ordered a general advance of all the armies of the United States upon the same date.

General McClellan, feeling that his own plan should be preferred, obtained permission from Mr. Lincoln to present his reasons therefor, in full; and in a letter prepared under date of February 3d, he reviewed the military situation at large and discussed in particular the two different lines of advance proposed for the army of the Potomac. The "best possible plan," in his judgment, he believed to be, to descend the Potomac, enter the Rappahannock, land at Urbana for a base, and by a rapid march gain West Point at the head of the York River; and thus threaten Richmond before John-

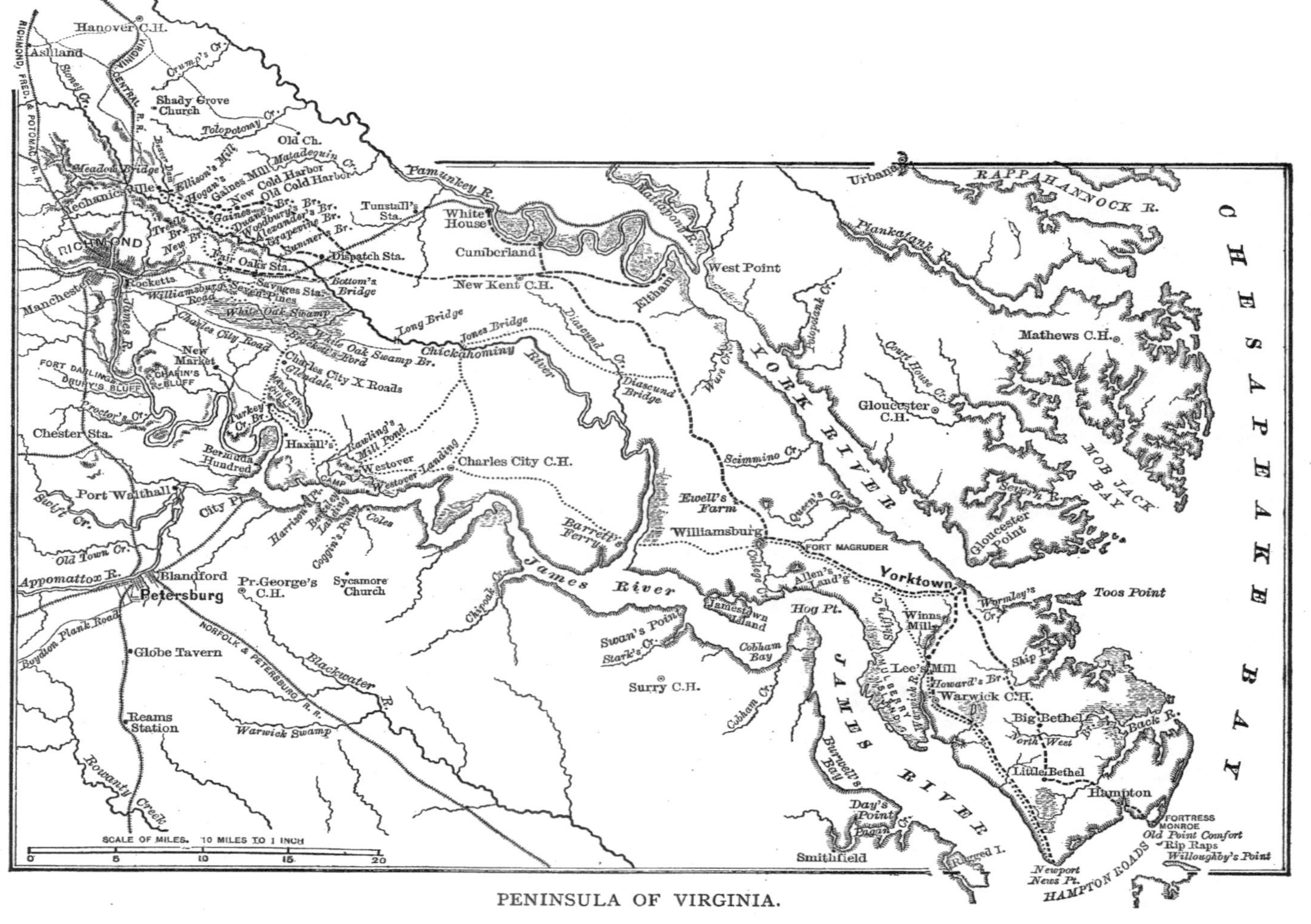

PENINSULA OF VIRGINIA.

ston's army at Centreville could fall back and meet him in condition to resist his progress. In other words, he proposed to outflank the enemy far on the left, and suddenly turn the tables by making the vicinity of Richmond and not Washington, the theatre of operations. This plan, he claimed, presented the shortest land route to the Confederate capital, and struck directly at the heart of the enemy's power at the East. Explaining further, he wrote: * "The total force to be thrown upon the new line would be, according to circumstances, from one hundred and ten thousand to one hundred and forty thousand. I hope to use the latter number by bringing *fresh troops* into Washington, and still leaving it quite safe. I fully realize that, in all projects offered, *time* will probably be the most valuable consideration. It is my decided opinion that in that point of view, the *second* plan should be adopted. It is possible—nay, highly probable, that the weather and state of the roads may be such as to delay the direct movement from Washington, with its unsatisfactory results and great risks, far beyond the time required to complete the second plan. In the first case, we can fix no definite time for an advance. The roads have gone from bad to worse. Nothing like their present condition was ever known here before; they are impassable at present. We are entirely at the mercy of the weather. It is by no means certain that we can beat them at Manassas. On the *other line* I regard success as certain by all the chances of war. We demoralize the enemy by forcing him to abandon his prepared position for one which we have chosen, in which all is in our favor, and where success must produce immense results. My judgment as a general is clearly in favor of this project. Nothing is cer-

* To Secretary Stanton.

tain in war, but all the chances are in favor of this movement. So much am I in favor of the southern line of operations, that *I would prefer the move from Fortress Monroe as a base,* as a certain though less brilliant movement than that from Urbana, to an attack upon Manassas. I know that the President and you and I all agree in our wishes, and that these wishes are to bring this war to a close as promptly as the means in our possession will permit. I believe that the mass of the people have entire confidence in us—I am sure of it. Let us then look only to the great result to be accomplished, and disregard everything else."

The merits of the Administration plan, on the other hand, as claimed by its advocates, lay in the fact, that a direct advance upon the enemy in front, first of all, kept the army between Washington and the rebels and rendered a counter attack upon the city impossible. This was a point of the greatest consequence. Washington, at all events, for sound political reasons, should be secured from insult and capture. The direct attack also involved a smaller expenditure of time and money; and in case of disaster, retreat could be effected with less difficulty.

Now, in regard to the Urbana plan, pronounced absurd by some of our best critics, we think that it was bold and not rash; that it was general and not limited. It was proved to be possible, if carried out as at first conceived. What principle of war is violated we are not prepared to discuss, unless we take time and space to show how little we applied such principles throughout the contest. In handling the army of the Potomac, our main principle was to secure Washington and take Richmond.

The rebels' principle was to take advantage, after they had had experience, of every demonstration of distrust or doubt of our ability to do that which would have been ordinarily done in war.

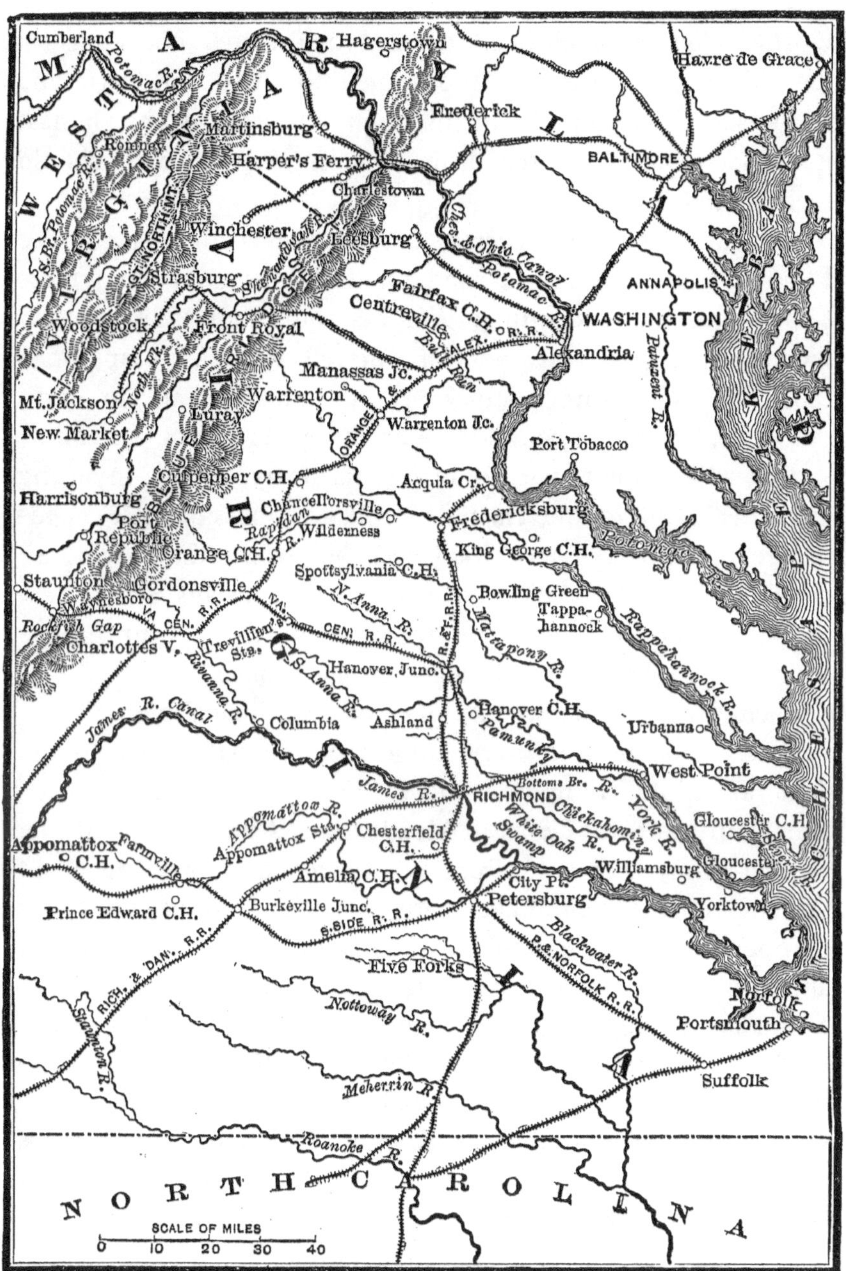

Field of Operations in Virginia.

This plan comprehended decided and active operations in the Shenandoah Valley; it designed to turn Yorktown and Gloucester; it ignored Norfolk and the use of the James; it carried with it all the dash of spirit a good plan should require and produce.

General McClellan became convinced that the enemy had 115,000 men at Manassas and on its flanks; and upon these false data, he determined that he could not take or turn those works. He was therefore driven to other plans than those involving direct attack. He did not prepare to carry out the plan proposed and endorsed by President Lincoln.

His sole object was to bring his army, as an invading army, as close to the enemy's capital as possible. He hoped to prevent unnecessary bloodshed; he expected to demoralize the enemy by rapid movements, bringing his army close to Richmond, to meet the rebels near that point before their troops should be "brought well in hand."

There was nothing in this plan new or impossible.

One of the best military authorities we have now living, General A. A. Humphreys, late Chief of Engineers, former Chief of Staff to General Meade, late Commander of the Second Army Corps in front of Richmond, was in favor of this movement. Combined with a strong and active series of operations in the valley, it threatened Richmond in rear and front, and *protected Washington;* and it would have forced a sudden attempt to bring about reconciliation and a patchwork peace from the rebels then and there, if our rulers were meek enough to make such a one. Some feared they were. They proved they were not. The fears of our best counsellors were transmitted to our generals. Politics entered and strategy retired.

The general commanding had conceived a plan which could have been carried out; and which would have placed us close to the city of Richmond in a very few days. He foresaw the trouble we afterward encountered by the direct route. He turned all the defences south of Urbana, and protected Washington, we repeat, through active operations directly upon Richmond; and more than all, he protected Washington by menacing the rebel communications with the West, through the operations in the valley of the Shenandoah.

It was absolutely impossible for the enemy to threaten Washington, even morally, if *he* were rapid and dashing in his movements. The movement to Urbana might have been the "stride of the giant."

Criticisms of this plan, based upon operations conducted in countries where every stream is well known, where every road is accurately mapped, and based upon so-called principles of war, cannot apply to this movement of new troops against new levies of insurgents, in a country of which but little was known to either of the commanding generals.

Finally, after many conferences, and the result of a council of war, wherein eight out of the twelve division commanders of the army reported in favor of McClellan's route by way of the lower Chesapeake, President Lincoln yielded his preference, and on March 8th, issued the following order:*

---

* The generals favoring the Administration plan were McDowell, Sumner, Heintzelman, and Barnard, the latter, Chief of Engineers. Those favoring the Urbana movement were Keyes, Franklin, Fitz-John Porter, W. F. Smith, McCall, Blenker, Andrew Porter, and Naglee, who represented Hooker. Keyes voted with the qualification that no change of base should be made until the Potomac was cleared of the rebel batteries.

The Committee on the Conduct of the War report that they had "no evidence, either oral or documentary, of the discussions that ensued, or the arguments that were submitted to the consideration of the President, that led him to relinquish his own line of operations, and consent to the one proposed by General McClellan, except the result of this Council of War."

PRESIDENT'S GENERAL WAR ORDER, NO. 3.

EXECUTIVE MANSION,
WASHINGTON, March 8, 1862.

Ordered, That no change of the base of operations of the Army of the Potomac shall be made without leaving in and about Washington such a force as, in the opinion of the General-in-Chief and the commanders of army corps, shall leave said city entirely secure.

That no more than two army corps (about fifty thousand troops) of said Army of the Potomac shall be moved en route for a new base of operations until the navigation of the Potomac from Washington to Chesapeake Bay shall be free from the enemy's batteries and other obstructions, or until the President shall hereafter give express permission.

That any movement as aforesaid, en route for a new base of operations, which may be ordered by the General-in-Chief, and which may be intended to move upon the Chesapeake Bay, shall begin to move upon the bay as early as the 18th of March instant; and the General-in-Chief shall be responsible that it so moves as early as that day.

Ordered, That the army and navy co-operate in an immediate effort to capture the enemy's batteries upon the Potomac, between Washington and the Chesapeake Bay.

ABRAHAM LINCOLN.

L. THOMAS, Adjutant-General.

On March 9th, the day after the issue of this order, the rebels *evacuated Centreville.*

This unexpected evacuation, General McClellan claims in his testimony before the Committee of Congress, to have been induced by information which reached the enemy while he was discussing his plans with the Administration. One reason why he had been so reserved was a mistrust that secrecy was not closely observed by others with whom he was obliged to have official communications. But General Johnston, on the other side, makes no admission that his movements were guided by espionage. He shows, in his

"Narrative," that the abandonment of Centreville had been contemplated for more than two weeks; and actually begun on March 7th, or the day before the promulgation of the President's order given above. Johnston's reasons for falling back and taking up a new position on the line of the Rappahannock are so fully expressed, that we quote his words: "We had to regard," he says, "four routes to Richmond as practicable for the Federal army: that chosen in the previous July [*via* Bull Run]; another east of the Potomac to the mouth of Potomac Creek, and thence by Fredericksburg; the third and fourth by water—the one to the Lower Rappahannock, the other to Fort Monroe; and from these points respectively by direct roads. As the Confederate troops in Virginia were disposed, it seemed to me that invasion by the second route would be the most difficult to meet; for as the march in Maryland would be covered by the Potomac, the Federal general might hope to conceal it from us until the passage of the river was begun, and so place himself at least two days' march nearer to Richmond than the Army of Northern Virginia on Bull Run. I did not doubt, therefore, that this route would be taken by General McClellan. The opinion was first suggested by the location of a division of the United States Army [Hooker's] opposite to Dumfries. On the 5th, information from Brigadier-General Whiting of unusal activity in the division opposite to him—that referred to above—suggested that the Federal army was about to take the field, so I determined to move to the position already prepared for such an emergency —the south bank of the Rappahannock, strengthened by field-works, and provided with a depot of food; for in it we should be better able to resist the Federal army advancing by Manassas, and near enough to Fredericksburg to meet the enemy there, should he take that route, as well as to unite with any

Confederate forces that might be sent to oppose him should he move by the Lower Rappahannock or Fort Monroe."*

By the 11th the entire rebel army had moved unmolested to the south bank of the Rappahannock, where Johnston fixed his headquarters near Rappahannock Station.

To but a single fact do we call attention in this connection: that during all the time that army lay at Centreville, insolently menacing Washington and frightening our civil and military authorities into the concentration of an enormous force around the city, it never presented an effective strength of over 50,000 men.†

With more than thrice that number, McClellan remained inactive for many precious weeks, under the delusion that he was confronted by a force very nearly equal to his own. It is astonishing that neither the General, nor the President, nor the searching Committee of Congress, nor the exacting Secretary of War, should have been able to ascertain the truth in the case during this long period. The only sources of intelligence upon which estimates seem to have been made, were the reports of deserters, contrabands, and country people who came into the lines, and underwent an examination at the hands of a detective at headquarters, who ranked upon the rolls as Chief of the Secret Service.

There now again arose the question, what was to be done? Upon hearing that the rebels had left his front, McClellan broke up his camps around the capital and marched toward Centreville, establishing himself at Fairfax Court House.

---

* Narrative of Military Operations Directed during the Late War between the States, p. 101. By Joseph E. Johnston, General C.S.A.

† The aggregate "present" in camp in Johnston's army for February, 1862, was 56,392; present for duty, 47,306. McClellan's aggregate, present for duty, for the same month was 150,000 in round numbers, excluding troops in the valley and in Maryland.

No wonder the Prince de Joinville describes the young general as appearing anxious and disturbed when directing this movement. To follow the enemy was deemed impracticable; to change the base seemed at this time to be the only plan which would give to the out-generalled army a chance to gain either reputation or increase of spirit.

General McClellan had left his headquarters in Washington, and might well be considered to have taken the field; and on March 11th, the President in another war order, relieved him of the command of all the military departments save the Department of the Potomac. Commanding from this period this army and department only, he confined his attention to active operations.

To repeat—what was to be done under the changed situation? Should the Urbana plan still be carried out?

To solve this new question, a council of war assembled at Fairfax Court House, March 13th, composed of the four Corps Commanders, Generals McDowell, Sumner, Heintzelman, and Keyes; before whom, in what seems to have been an informal conversation, General McClellan laid the proposition of moving further down the Chesapeake, and making Fort Monroe the base of operations.* This was at last the Peninsula plan, the third that had been considered, a kind of *"dernier ressort."* It had already been mentioned by McClellan, as a possible alternative, in his letter of February 3d, where he writes: "Should circumstances render it not advisable to land at Urbana, we can use Mob Jack Bay—or the worst coming to the worst, we can take Fort Monroe as a base, and operate with complete security, although with less celerity and brilliancy of results, up the Peninsula." The Urbana plan had been shorn of its merits and feasibility

* This council was summoned by General McClellan, not by the President.

since Johnston's retirement to the Rappahannock. McClellan now could not expect to steal a march upon him. There remained no other course but to take what the General describes as the safe route between the York and the James. That it was a route which had its advantages will not be denied. It was expected that West Point could be speedily reached at little sacrifice of life; and, as meditated in the Urbana plan, the scene of operations would thus be transferred to the immediate vicinity of Richmond. If the Urbana plan was a good one, as we thoroughly believe it to have been, there are substantial reasons for also regarding the Peninsula plan in a favorable light; securing, as it would have done, about the same, or at least, satisfactory results. Necessarily the approval of any plan must be premised upon the expected vigorous execution of it.

The corps commanders at the council of the 13th, although three of their number (McDowell, Sumner, and Heintzelman) had, as division commanders, disapproved the Urbana plan, adopted General McClellan's final Peninsula proposition, without dissent. Their proceedings were summed up as follows:

"HEADQUARTERS ARMY OF THE POTOMAC,
FAIRFAX COURT HOUSE, March 13, 1862.

"A council of the generals commanding army corps, at the headquarters of the Army of the Potomac, were of the opinion:

"I. That, the enemy having retreated from Manassas to Gordonsville, behind the Rappahannock and Rapidan, it is the opinion of generals commanding army corps that the operations to be carried on will be best undertaken from Old Point Comfort, between the York and James Rivers, provided, 1st, that the enemy's vessel, Merrimac, can be neutralized; 2d, that the means of transportation sufficient for an immediate transfer of the force to its new base can be ready at Washington and Alexandria to move down the Potomac; and 3d, that a naval auxiliary force can be had to silence, or aid in silencing the enemy's batteries on the York River; 4th, that the force to be left to cover Washington shall be such as to give an entire feeling of security for its safety from menace. (Unanimous.)

"II. If the foregoing cannot be, the army should then be moved against the enemy behind the Rappahannock at the earliest possible moment, and the means for reconstructing bridges, repairing railroads, and stocking them with materials for supplying the army should at once be collected for both the Orange and Alexandria and the Acquia and Richmond Railroads (unanimous). N. B.—That, with the forts on the right bank of the Potomac fully garrisoned, and those on the left bank occupied, a covering force in front of the Virginia line of twenty-five thousand men would suffice (Keyes, Heintzelman, and McDowell). A total of forty thousand men for the defence of the city would suffice (Sumner)."

This was approved by General McClellan, and immediately communicated to the War Department; and on the same day the following reply was received:

"WAR DEPARTMENT, March 13, 1862.

"The President, having considered the plan of operations agreed upon by yourself and the commanders of army corps, makes no objection to the same, but gives the following directions as to its execution:

"1. Leave such force at Manassas Junction as shall make it entirely certain that the enemy shall not repossess himself of that situation and line of communication.

"2. Leave Washington entirely secure.

"3. Move the remainder of the force down the Potomac, choosing a new base at Fortress Monroe, or anywhere between there and here; or at any event, move such remainder of the army at once in pursuit of the enemy by some route.

"EDWIN M. STANTON, Secretary of War.

"Major-General GEORGE B. MCCLELLAN."

But the council demanded a great deal more than it was ever possible to carry out. The whole position of affairs, as presented when General McClellan made known his first plans, had been changed by the appearance of the rebel ram Merrimac, or Virginia, on March 8th.* Although the navy had neutralized her power in so far as to prevent her injuring our new base, she still prevented us from utilizing the James River, and also demanded the diversion of a large portion of the naval forces to watch her, and prevented the admiral even from considering the practicability of running by the batteries at Yorktown or co-operating with the army in the movement up the Peninsula, had he been called upon so to do. General McClellan (page 118, Report) says: "The general plan, therefore, remained undisturbed, although less promising in its details than when the James River was in our control." Unfortunately, the fact was that we were now to work upon Plan No. 3, or the plan of the council, with the western flank of the Army of the Peninsula resting on the rebel gunboats, and not on the United States Navy.

Here, also, let us present one fatal consequence of McClellan's long dwelling on the Urbana plan, and his delay in executing it. He probably, little thought he would be driven to his *"dernier ressort"* for a base; and he committed a fatal error in leaving *Norfolk* to be turned.

Admiral Goldsborough, commanding the fleet in the lower Chesapeake, Assistant Secretary of the Navy G. V. Fox, and General J. G. Barnard had, as early as December, 1861, pointed out to General McClellan the necessity of his taking Norfolk. This rebel navy yard was in full blast, and the rebel rams and the Merrimac were growing, and threatening our navy and our transports. All that was required to secure to us the whole of their machinery, naval supplies, and their fleet, was a detachment of thirty or forty thousand

---

* The doings of the Merrimac and the subsequent gallant action of the Monitor are omitted here to preserve the continuity of the narrative. We must refer the reader to more extended works for the naval operations.

men. The capture of Norfolk would have changed everything. General McClellan probably believed that that place would fall through his own then contemplated movement; and he did nothing to carry out these views, so ably presented by our very best naval and military advisers.

Had he made the attempt and secured the success of this movement by a strong attack or feint threatening Manassas, the problem presented to the council of corps commanders would have been very different from the one they encountered at Fairfax Court House.

Nothing that was proposed or ordered, which contemplated making Fortress Monroe a base, had anything to do with General McClellan's first and only well-digested plan.

At this point we defer all further consideration of the campaign plans, and the plan finally adopted, for a brief review in the closing chapter. Why the Peninsula route was at length followed, we have seen. McClellan could not bring himself to adopt the Administration plan of a direct advance upon Centreville and the overland route to Richmond. Mr. Lincoln could not agree with the General in the choice of the Urbana base, but yielded his preferences; especially before the expressed opinion of the council of division commanders. Johnston suddenly moved and deranged the Urbana scheme; and McClellan and his corps commanders could fix upon nothing else than an advance upon Richmond by way of the Peninsula. To this the President gave his consent, under certain conditions; and it remained the final plan for the campaign.

When the plan had been adopted, the Secretary of War naturally required from General McClellan a detailed statement of his designs with regard to the employment of the

Army of the Potomac; and on March 19th the General gave to the Secretary, the following as these details: Fort Monroe was to be the base; the line of operations, that of Yorktown and West Point upon Richmond. A decisive battle was to be expected between West Point and Richmond. To succeed, he wished all the available forces to be collected at once, and to reach West Point as soon as possible, in order that he might establish his main depot there. To reach West Point he stated there were two methods: First, to move directly from Fortress Monroe with the main force, and to land troops near Yorktown, driving out the troops south of that point; then reduce Yorktown and Gloucester by a siege; second, to make a combined naval and land attack upon Yorktown, the first object of the campaign. To do this he required a concentration of all the most powerful batteries in the navy upon the York River; and he urged repeatedly, the necessity of the navy's throwing all its available force against Yorktown. Neither in this letter, nor in any communication that we can discover, did General McClellan intimate that he could carry out the orders of the Government with a smaller movable force than that he had first proposed; that is to say, 140,000 men.

Our unhappy campaign opened with a march to Centreville—a mere movement, calculated to rid the army of useless baggage, and fit it for embarkation for the new base. During this month, the transports which had previously been collected at Annapolis for the Urbana movement, were rapidly accumulating at Alexandria; but they did not assemble in numbers and capacity sufficient to transport, as General McClellan claims he was promised they would, 50,000 men at a time.

The embarkation began March 17th. Heintzelman's corps

led, Hamilton's division moving first; on the 22d Porter's followed, and the General placed both in position on roads leading to Newport News and to Yorktown. The rest of the army embarked as best it could. General McClellan left with his headquarters on the steamer Commodore, on April 1st, and

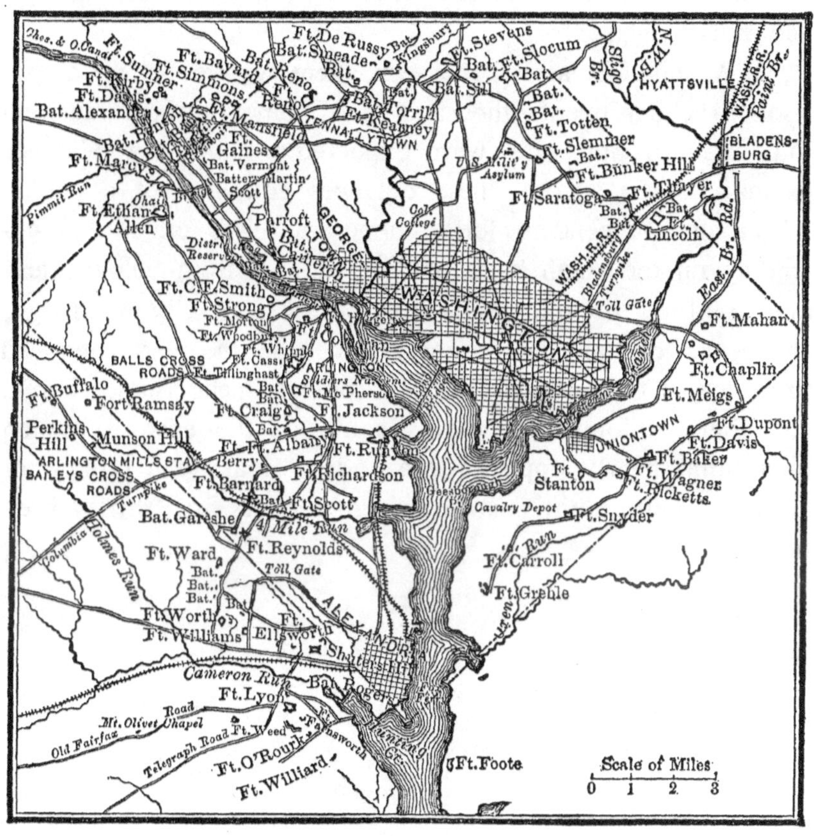

Washington and its Defences.

reached Fort Monroe on the afternoon of the 2d. He reports that he had at Fort Monroe and its vicinity, *ready to move,* two divisions of the Third Corps under General Heintzelman; two divisions of the Fourth, or Keyes' corps;

one division of the Second, or Sumner's corps; Sykes' regular infantry brigade; Hunt's reserve artillery, and three regiments of cavalry, in all about fifty-eight thousand men and one hundred guns. Casey's division of the Fourth Corps could not move without wagons, and Richardson's division of the Second, and Hooker's, of the Third Corps, had not arrived.

At Washington, as will be seen, there was to be left a garrison of about twenty thousand men, some of them raw and indifferent troops, who were expected to hold the defences against sudden attack. These defences consisted of a cordon of strong, independent forts, supporting each other, and extending on the south bank of the Potomac from below Alexandria along beyond Arlington Heights to Chain Bridge, above the capital. On the Maryland side the line continued from the Potomac to the eastern branch, near Bladensburgh, and thence along the heights south of the eastern branch to a point nearly opposite Alexandria—making a circuit, or "total development," as Barnard reports, of thirty-three miles.

CHAPTER III.

ACTIVE OPERATIONS. — SIEGE OF YORKTOWN.

IN entering upon the narrative of the active operations of the campaign, the two leading facts to be met and dealt with are:

First.—That while General McClellan succeeded in reaching the vicinity of his objective point—the Confederate capital—the results at each stage of his progress were inadequate and disappointing.

Second.—That when that point seemed to be within his grasp, his army suddenly encountered reverses, and retreated from its advanced position to the banks of the James.

The history of the campaign, in short, is the history of a lamentable failure—nothing less; and in presenting its features and incidents, the natural tendency will be to investigate fully and radically, so far as such a course is possible, those movements or delays upon which the failure apparently hinged. The point of interest must always necessarily be, to indicate and establish the responsibility in each case; whether that responsibility is found to rest with one individual or many, or with those unforeseen or uncontrollable agencies which are vaguely described as the "fortune of war," but which usually prove to be the superior ability or resources of the antagonist.

What, then, we ask, as a proper initial inquiry, were

General McClellan's intentions and immediate plan upon arriving to take the field from Fort Monroe?

He proposed the prompt, direct, and vigorous offensive. Upon this point there is no obscurity. "I had hoped," says the General in his report, "by rapid movements to drive before me or capture the enemy on the Peninsula, open the James River, and push on to Richmond before he should be materially reinforced from other portions of his territory." Entering into details, it will be observed that the plan contemplated the advance of the main body of the army up the Peninsula, with the co-operation of the navy in the rivers; while a powerful column, consisting of McDowell's First Corps, over 40,000 strong, was to operate upon the right, on either bank of the York, to turn the enemy's positions should they offer resistance on the direct route.* This was but a proposal to execute one of those large flank movements which met with such frequent success on both sides in the after-campaigns of the war. Under this plan it was expected that the advance of the army would be continuous, or at least be only briefly delayed, until West Point should be reached, where the base of immediate operations against Richmond was to be established.

But McClellan had not been on the Peninsula six days, before he experienced two serious disappointments—his plans suffered derangement in two important respects. In the first place, he ascertained upon his arrival at Fort Monroe that the navy would be unable to co-operate with him efficiently; and five days later the more surprising information was received, that McDowell's entire corps was detached from his command and ordered to remain in front of Wash-

* Referring to the First Corps, McClellan reports: ". . . . I intended to move it in mass to its point of disembarkation, and to land it on either bank of the York, as might then be determined."—Report, p. 73.

ington. Whether General McClellan was himself at fault in the case, and made his combinations upon insufficient assurance that he would receive all the assistance he expected, is a question to be considered; but the fact itself stands, that after entering upon the execution of his matured plans, he found them unexpectedly interrupted and requiring, as he believed; material modification.*

Now, as to the failure of the navy, or rather its non-co-operation, the question of responsibility turns upon the representations made to General McClellan before he left Washington. That he confidently anticipated its aid, is clear from what he says in proposing a combined naval and land attack upon Yorktown as the preliminary operation on the Peninsula. "To accomplish this," he wrote to Secretary Stanton, March 19th, "the navy should at once concentrate upon the York River all their available and most powerful batteries; its reduction should not in that case require many hours. A strong corps would be pushed up the York, under cover of the navy, directly upon West Point, immediately upon the fall of Yorktown, and we could at once establish our new base of operations at a distance of some twenty-five miles from Richmond; with every facility for developing and bringing into play the whole of our available force on either or both banks of the James. It is impossible to urge too strongly the absolute necessity of the *full co-operation of the navy* as a part of this programme."

So urgent was McClellan on this point, that on the same evening he telegraphed from Fairfax Court House to the Secretary as follows:

* "This army being reduced by forty-five thousand troops—some of them among the best in the service—and without the support of the navy, the plan to which we are reduced bears scarcely any resemblance to the one I voted for."—*General Keyes to Senator Harris:* McClellan's Report, p. 80.

"Please have an immediate decision upon the letter which will reach you to-morrow morning in regard to co-operation of the navy. That matter is important."

Mr. Stanton replied at once:

"In order to determine the precise co-operation you want with the navy, the President will go immediately to Alexandria, and desires you to meet him at the wharf."

The result of this interview, if it occurred, does not appear; but on that day, the 20th, McDowell was at Washington, and wrote the following to McClellan:

"Nothing decisive at the President's.

"The plan seemed to find favor with all who spoke. The only question seemed to be as to the ability of the navy to do their part. I am to go again in the morning when Barnard returns. Whether the navy can or not do anything, I think it evident they cannot before you can ship another division of Heintzelman's to Old Point. I spoke to the President, and he thought this would be best, so as not to keep the means of transportation idle. I would therefore send Heintzelman's second division at once, or as soon as you can. His first arrived safe last night and was landing. The Secretary says you should have no difficulty with Wool."

Three days before, on the 17th, McDowell had written this:

"In connection with General Barnard, I have had a long conference with the Assistant Secretary, Fox, as to naval co-operation. He promises all the power of the Department shall be at our disposal. At my suggestion he has told Commodore Goldsborough to confer with Colonel Woodbury concerning the plans now in view."

On the same day Mr. Welles, Secretary of the Navy, sent despatches to the commandants of the navy yards at New York and Boston, to send what gunboats they had ready "to Hampton Roads at once."* Furthermore, General

* The despatches quoted appear on file in the War and Navy Departments.

Barnard went down to Hampton Roads, to consult Commodore Goldsborough, but it would appear from the latter's testimony, that the question of breaking through between Yorktown and Gloucester was not discussed.

From the foregoing despatches, it is evident that McClellan cannot be charged with not having pressed the matter of naval co-operation upon the attention of the Government.

On the other hand, how did the naval authorities understand this plan of co-operation with the army? If General McClellan was distinctly informed, as stated by himself, that the navy would assist him as he desired, it is impossible to assume that either the Secretary of the Navy or the officer commanding the fleet in Hampton Roads would not have known the fact, and been impressed with his needs and expectations.

The naval authorities, on the contrary, claim to have received no intimation that any *special* co-operation, in the way of a difficult attempt, was required of them. The testimony of Mr. Fox, Assistant Secretary of the Navy, and of Admiral Goldsborough, commanding the Hampton Roads fleet, is conclusive as to this. Mr. Fox, for instance, was asked by Mr. Gooch:

Question.— "Do you know whether or not it was expected that the navy should take the batteries of the enemy at or about Yorktown?"

Anyswer.—"I never heard that it was."

Question.—"Was that feasible?"

Answer.—"Not to attack those batteries. Wooden vessels could not have attacked the batteries at Yorktown and Gloucester with any degree of success. The forts at Yorktown were situated too high; were beyond the reach of naval guns; and I understood that General McClellan never expected any attack to be made upon them by the navy."

And to a previous question he had replied in the same vein: "So far as I know, all the vessels that General McClellan required in his operations against Yorktown, were placed at his disposal by Admiral Goldsborough. I am not aware that he ever required that we should attack Yorktown; or that it was ever expected that we should do so."

Admiral Goldsborough's testimony is still more emphatic:

Question.—"What part was the navy called upon to act in the campaign of the Peninsula, as it is called?"

Answer.—"With regard to that campaign, no naval authority whatever, to my knowledge, was ever consulted until after a considerable part of the army got down there. The whole matter was arranged here in Washington by officers in the army, as I understood. I believe they never said a word, even to the Secretary of the Navy. Certainly, nothing was ever said to me until the eleventh hour. Then it was that I heard that they expected the navy to co-operate with them. The Assistant Secretary of War, Mr. Watson, came down to see me in behalf, as he said, of the Secretary of War and the President of the United States. He told me of the great anxiety felt in Washington in regard to the Merrimac; that they were apprehensive she might get up the York River and entirely disconcert all the movements of the army. I told Mr. Watson that the President might make his mind perfectly easy about the Merrimac going up York River; that she never could get there, for I had ample means to prevent that. This was in the latter part of March, 1862. The army at that time was about assembling at Old Point Comfort. General McClellan had not then arrived."

The Admiral goes on further to declare, that he did everything that the General requested of him—detailing seven gunboats for his purposes, being all the former wanted; and adds that, upon the day of his arrival off Fort Monroe and before going ashore, the General came on board of his ship to consult with him "as to the best mode of attacking Yorktown." This mode contemplated a flank attack by way of the Severn River upon the Gloucester works; on the fall of which, the gunboats could run by Yorktown and render that position untenable,

These extracts from the testimony before the Committee on the Conduct of the War, are introduced for the single purpose of testing the charge that the navy is to be held responsible for causing the first serious derangement of McClellan's campaign plan. The navy was clearly ignorant of the scope and intent of that plan; was not a party to it; had not promised to join in a combined attack upon Yorktown, and moreover, could probably have effected nothing in such an attempt.*

*The files of the Navy Department contain no orders in the matter. At a later date, April 15th, Secretary Welles sent the following to Admiral Goldsborough, the tenor of which hardly warrants the inference that he had previously despatched more specific instructions:

"*Sir*—The attention of the whole country, as well as of the Department, is turned with intense interest at this time to the naval and army movements in Lower Virginia. I commend your determination not to be drawn into a conflict where the enemy can take you at disadvantage, and would enjoin unceasing vigilance at every point. It cannot be many days before the Galena, which is now receiving her armament on board, will be with you, and will, I trust, prove an efficient acquisition to your squadron. Your determination. should the enemy shell Newport News, not to be drawn among the shoals and narrow waters thereabouts, seems to me wise and proper.

"You will actively and earnestly co-operate with Major-General McClellan, whose position and movements at Yorktown and on York River are of momentous interest and consequence to the whole country. Any and all aid that you can render him and the army you will extend at all times. It is important and absolutely essential that he should secure all the assistance that he may require of the navy and that it is in your power to bestow consistently with your other duties.

"The general objects and designs of the Government and the great interests dependent on the naval and army movements in the vicinity of Hampton Roads are well understood by you.

"In addition to the general facts from time to time communicated to you, the

The whole explanation of the matter seems to be, that while General McClellan expressed his profound anxiety that the navy should render its aid, he expected more than the Government could promise or the navy accomplish. If he was disappointed to find at Fort Monroe that the gunboats were not to batter down and run by Yorktown, we must assume that it was because he had not assured himself before leaving Washington that that particular service could be and was to be performed by them. The General distinctly intimated that he should depend upon them to reduce the place, but it remains to be shown by evidence which has not come within our reach, whether he had been promised that they would. To us it appears that McClellan meant one thing by "co-operation," and that the navy, then absorbed with the Merrimac, and not impressed with the scope of his expectations, meant another.

The nature of General McClellan's second disappointment —the retention of McDowell's corps—and who was there at fault, will be presently noticed in its proper connection.

Compelled to forego all thought of valuable assistance from the navy, McClellan, depending now entirely upon his

---

Assistant Secretary of the Navy has visited you on your station and made known the wishes of the Government in person.

"Whether and to what extent you can detach any portion of your command from their employment on other stations at this juncture, I am unable to decide. To your judgment these and other matters are confided with a solicitude and anxiety I cannot express, but with a confidence that the country will not be disappointed in you.

"I am, respectfully,
"Your ob't servant,
"GIDEON WELLES.

"Flag Officer L. M. GOLDSBOROUGH,
"Command'g N. A. Block'g Squad.,
"Hampton Roads, Va."

[From the MS. Records, Navy Department.]

army, modified his plans to a certain extent. The modification, however, does not prove to have been radical. No important change was made. He proceeded with the original idea—an advance of the main army up the Peninsula, with a flanking column on the right. The only deviation appears in the fact that whereas, before, the navy was expected to attack and reduce Yorktown without delay, and continue to turn all the enemy's positions on the York, this work was now to be done somewhat more slowly by McDowell's flanking column, moving up the left bank of that river.

In other words, General McClellan's initial plan, adopted at and undertaken from Fort Monroe, was this: to move forward, first, in two columns with the troops already disembarked—one column marching on the right direct to Yorktown, and another along the James River westward of and beyond Yorktown to the vicinity of Williamsburg. Then, to use the General's own words, it was designed, "should the works at Yorktown and Williamsburg offer serious resistance, to land the First Corps (McDowell's), reinforced if necessary, on the left bank of the York or on the Severn, to move it on Gloucester and West Point, in order to take in reverse whatever force the enemy might have on the Peninsula, and compel him to abandon his positions." From this it will be seen, that whatever obstacles the main army met with in marching to Richmond, or the base at West Point, they were all to be turned by McDowell. Delay in carrying these positions would thus be overcome and preliminary losses avoided. The plan was based on sound military principles.

The movement forward began on April 4th. The column directed against Yorktown included the Third Corps—Porter's and Hamilton's divisions only having arrived—Sedgwick's division of the Second Corps, and Averill's Third

Pennsylvania Cavalry, under General Heintzelman. The column on the left, commanded by General Keyes, was composed of the divisions of Smith and Couch, of the Fourth Corps, with the Fifth Regular Cavalry temporarily attached. The transportation of Casey's division, of the Fourth, not being disembarked, it remained in camp at Newport News, from which point the left column started. The columns marched from ten to twelve miles and bivouacked at night at Young's Mills on the left, near the James, and on the right at Howard's Bridge and Cockletown beyond. The enemy showed themselves on the right; but offered no serious resistance. The reserve, consisting of Hunt's artillery, Stoneman's cavalry, and Sykes' brigade of regular infantry, encamped at Big Bethel.

At six o'clock on the following morning, the 5th, the march was resumed. Heintzelman received orders to advance with the Third Corps to a point two and three-fourths miles from Yorktown; while Keyes was instructed to continue on the left, by way of Warwick Court House, to an old landmark known as the "Half-way House," between Yorktown and Williamsburg. The orders to Keyes, which will be presently noticed, were significant; requiring him to occupy and hold "the narrow dividing ridge near the Half-way House, so as to prevent the escape of the garrison at Yorktown by land, and prevent reinforcements being thrown in." Had these orders been executed to the letter, and the left column especially been able to reach and hold the point indicated, on the evening of the 5th, the Commanding General would have had the satisfaction of reporting most substantial progress made "up the Peninsula" during these first two days.

But hardly had the army filed into the roads for the march of the 5th, before it encountered that series of fatalities which were to be its almost daily experience through this disheartening campaign. To follow the column under Keyes, whose immediate success was of most importance, we find that general sending word to headquarters just as Smith's division was moving out, "6 A.M.," that, from the best information he could obtain, a large force of the enemy was occupying a strong position, defended by three guns, at Lee's Mills, six miles beyond on the road he was following. "It is my opinion," he said, "that we shall encounter very serious resistance; if so, we shall not be able to reach the Half-way House on the Yorktown and Williamsburg road to-day. . . . I respectfully suggest that a strong reserve force be within my reach. . . . Our wagons did not arrive last night, and we shall be obliged to halt at Warwick Court House for the infantry reserve ammunition to come up. . . . It is a heavy march to the Half-way House, even without opposition." At half-past seven he added: "The roads are very bad ahead. Shall I push on to Half-way House if artillery cannot get on fast enough? I suppose not, of course." And again, at 3 P.M., he reports: "I am stopped by the enemy's works at Lee's Mills, which offer a severe resistance; the road through the woods for nearly a mile having become absolutely impassable for artillery, I am cutting a new road through. One battery is replying to the enemy, and another is nearly or quite through."

The rain had been falling in torrents all the morning; and it was not until about noon that the advance, under Keyes, struck the enemy's skirmishers. Hancock's brigade, of Smith's division, deployed on the right, Davidson's on the left, and Brooks' in reserve. Couch's division rested at Warwick Court House, with part of Peck's and Graham's brigades, extended down the Warwick River. Finding the march thus seriously obstructed at Lee's Mills, the column encamped for the night in the above order.

Upon the right, Heintzelman was also stopped; but that was expected, his march being upon Yorktown. From Cockletown, Porter's division moved forward on the 5th, with Morell's brigade in advance—Berdan's Independent Regiment of Sharpshooters taking the lead—and after a march of three miles, came under the fire of the enemy's works. It happened to be at the point designated by General McClellan, where this column was to halt for further orders, and General Morell thus describes the preliminary incidents in his report to General Porter: "At seven o'clock on the morning of the 5th, we were again in motion, the cavalry still in the rear. The rain commenced falling at the same time, which made the road exceedingly heavy, and delayed our progress. You joined me at the saw-mill, your staff and mine forming a conspicuous group; and at 10 A.M., as we arrived at the junction of the Warwick with the Yorktown road, we received the first shot from the enemy. It came from their works on our right near the town, and was well aimed, though a little too high. The sharpshooters, under Colonel Berdan, were alone in front of us." "Looming up in the mist and rain," says General Porter at the same time, "were extensive defences of the enemy, from which we were immediately saluted with the fire of artillery." Porter at once made his dispositions: Morell deploying in front and supporting Weeden's and Griffin's batteries, which opened upon the enemy's works at a distance of two thousand yards, and Martindale's brigade, at one o'clock, taking position on the left of Morell's, with Butterfield's brigade in reserve. Artillery firing and some skirmishing occurred with little loss during the afternoon; and at night, the division encamped on the ground fronting the works at Yorktown and those connecting on its right.

The position, then, of McClellan's army, on the morning

3

of the 6th, was not that contemplated in his orders for the 5th. Keyes, certainly, should have been at the Half-way House, near Williamsburg. But he had met an obstruction. His progress on the 5th was five miles—no more; Porter's, four. Right here begins that month's delay at Yorktown. One thing is certain: it was not strategic delay—delay for a purpose, since the General had promised rapid movements forward, and had provided flank operations to expedite the direct. What, then, caused it? Could not and ought not the delay to have been avoided? Let us look at this carefully and impartially.

Preliminary to these questions, it should be ascertained what the enemy had been doing on the Peninsula, and what precisely was their position on the 5th, when resistance by them first proved serious.

The Confederate attitude in this quarter had been, from the first, that of defence. For some time after the affair of Big Bethel, June 10, 1861, they had made Yorktown their base of observation, with posts thrown out several miles in advance. Major-General J. Bankhead Magruder, late of the United States Army, commanded. By March 1, 1862, Magruder had laid out, and partially completed, three defensive lines across the Peninsula, from Williamsburg down toward Fort Monroe. What he proposed and describes as his "real line of defence positions," was the one at the front, seven miles below Yorktown; or at that point between Howard's and Young's Mills, where the setting back of the Poquosin River from the York and the mouths of the Warwick and Deep Creek, on the James, contract the intervening solid ground to the short distance of three miles. "Both flanks of this line," says Magruder, "were defended by boggy and difficult streams and swamps. In addition, the left flank was defended by elaborate fortifications at

Ship Point, connected by a broken line of redoubts crossing the heads of the various ravines emptying into York River and Wormley's Creek, and terminating at Fort Grafton, nearly in front of Yorktown. The right flank was defended by the fortifications at the mouth of Warwick River and at Mulberry Island Point, and the redoubts extending from the Warwick to James River. Intervening between the two mills was a wooded country, about two miles in extent. This wooded line, forming the centre, needed the defence of infantry in a sufficient force to prevent any attempt on the part of the enemy to break through it. In my opinion, this advanced line, with its flank defences, might have been held by 20,000 troops. With 25,000 I do not believe it could have been broken by any force the enemy could have brought against it. Its two flanks were protected by the Virginia (Merrimac) and the works on one side, and the fortifications at Yorktown and Gloucester Point on the other."

His force being reduced by detachments sent across the James to Suffolk and Portsmouth, Magruder abandoned this advanced line about March 1st, and fell back to his second line, running from Yorktown on his left along the Warwick River to Mulberry Island, and the James upon the right. The third line, to be noticed later, was that constructed in front of Williamsburg, eleven miles farther up the Peninsula. His second, or the Yorktown position, was, in point of extent, the least defensible of the three; but it presented the counterbalancing advantage of having its left protected by the projecting bank of the York at Gloucester, whose works, in conjunction with those at Yorktown opposite, were expected to close the river to the passage of the Union gun-boats.*

---

* The Count de Paris in his well known and admirable work, states that Magruder persisted in holding the Yorktown position in spite of orders from Richmond to abandon it. I find no confirmation of this statement, but infer from

Although embracing a front of "twelve miles," as Magruder reports, this line had been converted by various fortifications and devices into a considerable barrier. Around Yorktown itself, the old embankments thrown up by the British in 1781, were substantially revived; and, at commanding positions outside of the village, two works were constructed, known as the "red" and "white" redoubts, united by long curtains. In the vicinity and to the west of these, or a mile and a half from Yorktown, the Warwick River takes its rise and flows in a southerly direction to the James. Its upper part, originally known as Beaverdam Creek, is described by Magruder as a "sluggish and boggy stream," twenty or thirty yards wide in some places, and running through "a dense wood fringed by swamps." There were two mills with dams upon its banks, one—Wynne's Mill—about three miles from Yorktown; the other—Lee's Mills—two and one-half miles below, where the James River road crosses the stream. Three additional dams were constructed by the enemy, making five in all; which had the effect of backing up the water and rendering its passage impracticable for either artillery or infantry, for nearly three-fourths of the distance. So, at least, reports Magruder. Each dam was covered by artillery and earthworks; while along the rear of the line, ran a recently opened military road. At Lee's Mills, strong fortifications had been erected, and from that point, the line presented a refused right, turning across Mulberry Island to Skiff Creek. The Confederate force defending this position, numbered 11,000 strong at the time McClellan moved forward from Fort Monroe, 6,000 defending the flanks at Yorktown and Mulberry Island,

what both Davis and Johnston say, and from Magruder's own report, that he was expected to dispute every inch of the Peninsula—the retention of Norfolk depending on his position.

and 5,000 posted at the dams and assailable points along the Warwick front.*

The existence of this line, in front of which he was brought to a halt on April 5th, was unknown to General McClellan. Both in the report of his operations and in his testimony before the Committee on the Conduct of the War, he refers to the lack of precise information respecting the topography of the Peninsula, as an element of delay and confusion in his movements. "Our maps," he testifies, "proved entirely inaccurate, and did us more harm than good, for we were constantly misled by them." Again, in his report, he observes: "The country, though known in its general features, we found to be inaccurately described in essential particulars in the only maps and geographical memoirs or papers to which access could be had. Erroneous courses to streams and roads were frequently given, and no dependence could be placed on the information thus derived. . . . Reconnoissances, frequently under fire, proved the only trustworthy sources of information." Heintzelman, Keyes, and other officers, mention the same want; and the inconvenience and difficulties arising from it.

* Colonel Cabell, of the Confederate artillery, reported May 10, 1862, as follows in regard to this position: "Three roads led up from the Peninsula and crossed the line of our defences. The first on our right was the Warwick road, that crossed at Lee's Mills; the second crossed at Wynne's Mill, and the third was commanded by the reboubts (Nos. 4 and 5) near Yorktown. The crossing at Lee's Mills was naturally strong, and fortifications had been erected there and at Wynne's Mill. Below Lee's Mills the Warwick River, affected by the tides and invested by swamps on each side, formed a tolerable protection; but the marshes could easily be made passable and the river bridged. Between Lee's and Wynne's Mills an unbroken forest extended on the right bank of the stream to a distance of about three miles. Two additional dams were constructed, the one (Dam No. 1) nearest to Wynne's Mill, and the other, Dam No. 2. A dam called the upper dam was constructed in the stream above Wynne's Mill. This detailed description of the line of defence seems necessary to explain the position of the artillery of the Peninsula."

But this was to have been anticipated. The Virginia Peninsula, like many portions even of the older States, was practically *terra incognita* for military purposes. Careful surveys of its entire extent had never been made, and when the topographical engineers set to work to construct maps for General McClellan's guidance, in view of his possible movement by that route, their results were necessarily insufficiently full or precise. Major-General A. A. Humphreys, then at the head of the Topographical Corps, consulted every available authority and record bearing upon the features of that region; and this information was used by the Commanding General. Among other maps brought to light, were the British plans of the siege of Yorktown, in 1781, and the original survey of the Peninsula from Fort Monroe to Williamsburg, made in 1818 by Major James Kearney, of the corps of Topographical Engineers, both of which satisfactorily established certain points. Various outlines were compiled; but the most elaborate, so far as it went, and the one followed by General McClellan, was that furnished by Lieutenant-Colonel T. J. Cram, then serving as engineer and aid-de-camp to General Wool, at Fort Monroe, which embraced Norfolk, Suffolk, and the Peninsula as far as the Half-way House above Yorktown. And yet this map, which, in view of its source, appears to have been regarded as the most reliable, was found to be in error in several important particulars, especially in indicating the course of the Warwick; which it represented as running nearly parallel with the road up the Peninsula, instead of running across it to the vicinity of Yorktown. Kearney's survey, on the other hand, indicates the true *direction* of the stream; but gives it no prominence as an impediment. With these maps before him, it is clear that McClellan did not expect to find the extensive line of defence which, as we have seen, Magruder had constructed and occupied. Thus, to the question asked by the Committee on the Conduct of the War,—whether he knew of the enemy's works before he landed on the Peninsula, McClellan replied: "No; we did not know of the line of works along the Warwick. We knew that Yorktown itself was surrounded by a continuous line of earthworks, but we did not know of the line of the Warwick. . . . When we did advance, we found the enemy intrenched and in strong force wherever, we approached. The nature and extent of his position along the Warwick River was not known to us when we left Fort Monroe."

How far a general may base the delay or failure of his movements on the meagreness and inaccuracy of his topographical information, depends upon the given case. General McClellan's situation in this respect, was probably but little different from that of other generals in other parts of the field. It was a war in which he who pushed and found out for himself, was the most likely to achieve results. In this particular instance, we may be permitted to quote from General Humphreys, that the information collected by his corps, in advancing up the Peninsula, "was quite as full as anything we had in the pursuit of Lee in April, 1865, after we got ten miles from Petersburg—indeed, more full, more complete."*

But, aside from the inadequate and misleading maps—aside, in fact, from the alleged non-co-operation of the navy, an important criticism is here suggested. Was this advance from Fort Monroe toward Yorktown itself, conducted upon correct tactical principles? Was it based upon a proper appreciation of the enemy's probable dispositions and foresight?

---

* Letter from General Humphreys to the writer, June, 1881.

Two things are beyond dispute: the published maps presented an accurate *outline* of the Peninsula—that is, the lines of the James and York; and, second, McClellan advanced upon the enemy in expectation of meeting resistance at Yorktown. As to the latter point, he states in his report, that, as he had ascertained that the Confederate General Huger could readily reinforce Magruder from Norfolk, and had already done so, and that Johnston's army could be rapidly transferred from Manassas to Yorktown, he proposed "to invest that town without delay." Cram's map, says McClellan, indicated "the feasibility of the design;" and from Fort Monroe the General hurried forward to execute it before the enemy could be reinforced. This was to be the first of the promised "rapid movements" toward Richmond.

By the courtesy of General H. G. Wright, the present Chief of the Corps of Topographical Engineers, the author is placed in possession of all the requisite official maps covering this campaign, inclusive of tracings of those by Kearney and Cram; and it is to be admitted, that according to the latter, Yorktown stands in a dangerously isolated situation, inviting attack, being apparently fortified for no other purpose than to close the York River in connection with the Gloucester works, and having no relation to the Peninsula as a defence against the approach of an army by land. To the uneducated eye, it seems to be a most "feasible" manœuvre to march to its rear, surround and invest it, and thus repeat what Washington effected upon the same spot in 1781, or what Grant enforced at Vicksburg in 1863. That General McClellan expected, upon the strength of Cram's map, to be able to surround Yorktown, is not only evident from his report, but, as we have already noticed, his orders to Keyes on April 5th, to march and encamp at the Half-way

House, six miles in the rear of Yorktown, indicate no misgivings on his part as to Keyes' ability to reach that point without much, if any, resistance.

But General McClellan's expectations here, were clearly too sanguine. Sound military judgment would have pronounced at once, that Keyes could not reach the Half-way House, nor any point to the rear of Yorktown, without the most obstinate resistance; and that, if that resistance had been overcome, the Confederates would have immediately abandoned the town. It was correctly presumed, that Magruder's purpose was to delay McClellan's progress up the Peninsula as long as possible. But did not this require him to present a front entirely *across* the Peninsula? What would it have availed to hold the road up the York and leave that along the James unguarded? Did McClellan expect that Magruder would shut himself up within the "continuous line of earthworks" around Yorktown, and suffer the former to throw a heavy column in his rear and thus prevent his escape? The moment Keyes reached the Half-way House, Magruder would be doomed. And yet it appears that the advance from Fort Monroe was based and hurried, upon this very anticipation. It will be observed, for instance, that McClellan reports himself as being surprised to learn that Keyes was checked in his march on April 5th. "*Unexpectedly*," he says, Keyes was brought to a halt before the enemy's works at Lee's Mills.

Now, on the contrary, just such a halt *ought to have been expected*. Nothing less than a continuous front of opposition from the York to the James should have been looked for. The existence of a strong fortified post at Yorktown, necessitated and implied the existence of an equally strong barrier at the other flank on the James, at or about Lee's Mills, with the intervening centre also defended. General Magruder, on the other side, certainly felt the necessity. "Deeming it *of vital importance*," he reports, "to hold Yorktown, on York River, *and* Mulberry Island, on James River, and to keep the enemy in check by an intervening line, until the authorities might take such steps as should be deemed

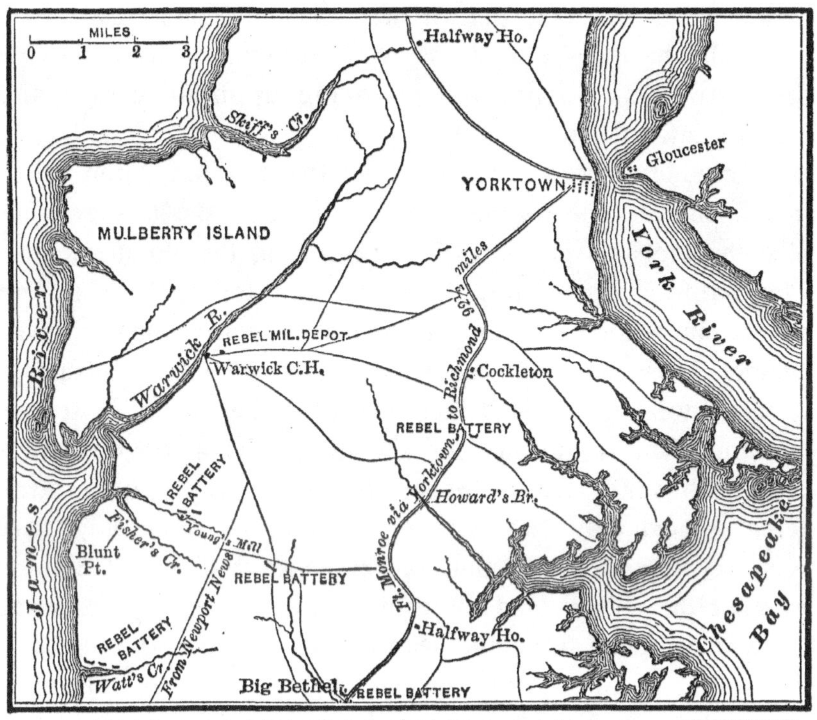

The "Cram" map.

necessary to meet a serious advance of the enemy on the Peninsula, I felt compelled to dispose my forces in such a manner as to accomplish these objects with the least risk possible, under the circumstances of great hazard which surrounded the little army I commanded." Cram's map erroneously places Warwick Court House on the Warwick River, where Lee's Mills should be, the latter not being indicated at all, and describes it simply as a "rebel military depot," eight or ten miles distant from Yorktown. That it is gravely misleading in its representation of the Confederate situation and the topography in that vicinity, is not to be denied. But the fact that it was accepted as correct, and made the basis of operations, when obviously it was to be discredited as a compilation made upon uncertain and meagre information, is open to the criticism suggested.

If blunders were committed in the advance upon Richmond, this may be regarded as the first one: the failure to divine the probable position of the enemy at the Yorktown line. The natural desire and determination to reach it before they were reinforced, was, unfortunately, unaccompanied with a right appreciation of the true method of taking advantage of their weakness. McClellan estimated the enemy's strength at about fifteen thousand; his own, at the start, was fifty-eight thousand. He proposed to use this preponderating force immediately and with effect; and it could only have been so used, by expecting to find a long defensive line in front of the enemy, and marching with a view of discovering its weakest point with the least possible delay, and breaking through it at once. But, instead, we find surprise at meeting with opposition—halt, and uncertainty.

In advancing these criticisms, it is true, a certain modification is to be made in General McClellan's favor. His plan of campaign did not require absolutely precise information of the enemy's position at Yorktown, or anywhere else on the Peninsula, with the view of overcoming it. That plan already provided for the obstacle of the Warwick. If anything like it existed, and could not readily be forced, it was to be *turned*. Whatever obstruction the main force on the Peninsula encountered, McDowell was expected to outflank it on the other side of the York. So that, while McClellan blundered in his expectations of surrounding Yorktown, his general plan remained feasible. The Warwick, in the execution of the latter, should have delayed him but a few days. Magruder would have retreated on learning of McDowell's march along the York to the White House in his rear.

It is at this point that we reach McClellan's second disappointment in the campaign—the retention of McDowell's corps at Washington.

The facts here may be briefly summarized as follows: One of the conditions on which the President approved the Peninsula plan, was, that Washington should be left completely secure against attack; and the council of corps commanders on March 13th, had named a force of about 55,000 men as necessary for this purpose. Upon McClellan's departure, General Wadsworth, the Military Governor of the city, reported that he could muster scarcely 20,000 troops for its defence in case of an emergency. Apparently alarmed that so scanty a force had been left, President Lincoln directed, on April 3d, that either McDowell's or Sumner's Corps, which had not all embarked for the new base, should be retained in front of Washington. It was claimed that McClellan had not complied with the condition above referred to, and that the retention of part of his own force was necessary for the safety of the capital. In his report the General ventures the defence, that he had left the prescribed number of troops; but we find that he includes among them the force under Banks, in the Shenandoah—a force which he regarded as a movable column thrown out for the defence of the capital. The corps commanders at the council did not so regard Banks, but fixed the 55,000 men for Washington as over and above what the latter commanded. In this light it is to be admitted that McClellan had failed to comply with President Lincoln's "explicit directions" and the decision of the council; and in view of the well-known feeling of the Government respecting the safety of the city, and the fact that the not over-friendly Committee of Congress watched every step he took, it is strange that the General should have given even the semblance of an opportunity to be interfered with, after once taking the field. A grave mistake it was, when he left Washington without having the President's assurance that all was well at least there.

That the withholding of McDowell was a shock to McClellan is certain. The news reached him on the 5th, conveyed in a brief telegram from the Adjutant-General, at the very moment when the Warwick was discovered to be a considerable obstruction; and when the necessity of a flanking column was immediately obvious. Right in the emergency, that column was withheld from his control; and we affirm, that, looking at the matter irrespective of every political bias, no matter how far McClellan's alleged disregard of instructions in leaving Washington unprotected, may have been true—no matter what the alarm of the commander of the Washington defences, or of the President's military advisers—either McClellan should have been relieved, or else every possible effort should have been made to keep his force, now actively engaged in the field, at the full strength with which alone he proposed to undertake his operations. Whether his own view was correct or incorrect, in that view he was crippled. He proposed a plan with McDowell as a principal actor in it. McDowell withdrawn, the plan was radically interfered with.

Writers have said that McClellan had none but himself to blame. Granted. But who shall be blamed for permitting a situation which, at all hazards, should just then have been avoided? If McClellan was still retained, one duty was incumbent upon the Government: it should have suffered at least half of McDowell's corps to proceed to the Peninsula at once, and then made every effort to reinforce the capital from other points. To allow the General to remain in command and then cut off the very arm with which he was about to strike, we hold to have been inexcusable and unmilitary to the last degree.

Leaving this question as, perhaps, the leading point of dispute in the campaign, and one which may never be satisfactorily set at rest, there come up all those various speculations indulged in by critics, respecting the course McClellan ought to have pursued after losing McDowell. A general of high spirit and sensitive soul might have found in the Government's action the occasion for sending in his resignation. Another, deeply earnest in the national behalf, might have suddenly roused himself to great exertions, and proved by successful strokes that he was worthy of the fullest confidence. General McClellan continued in command, accepted the situation, and endeavored to make the best of it.

What to do—was now the question. It has been claimed that the General should have immediately forced the Warwick, and effected the capture or compelled the evacuation of Yorktown—thus opening the York River and securing the White House as a base. That the Warwick line could have been readily broken within a week after the army's arrival before it, we now know. McClellan at the time was of a different opinion; although but a few days before he had calculated the relative forces at 58,000 against 15,000. In explanation he testified that Johnston arrived opposite to him the same evening that he reached the Yorktown front, April

5th, implying that the rebel army lately at Manassas was now again in his front. The General's information-based, by the way, on altogether insufficient, if not unreliable data —was erroneous. Johnston did not arrive in person to supersede Magruder until after the 14th; and of his army, the advance division, under General D. H. Hill, did not arrive at Yorktown until the 10th; the other divisions following a few days later. For six days at least, after McClellan appeared in front of the Warwick, he was fully three times stronger than the enemy in point of numbers.

But here again, it is to be admitted that McClellan presented plausible reasons-reasons already referred to—for not attempting a direct attack on Magruder's position at that time. The General, despite the retention of McDowell, still clung to his original plan (modified slightly) of flanking the enemy. It was a plan adopted after long deliberation; and he was wholly unwilling to abandon it, though seemingly deprived of the means of its execution. Thus, when President Lincoln urged him, April 6th, to break the line of the 'Warwick at once; McClellan replied: "Under the circumstances that have been developed since we arrived here, I feel fully impressed with the conviction, that here is to be fought the great battle that is to decide the existing contest. I shall, of course, commence the attack as soon as I can get up my siege-train, and shall do all in my power to carry the enemy's works; but, to do this with a reasonable degree of certainty, requires, in my judgment, that I should, if possible, have at least the whole of the First Army Corps (McDowell's) to land upon York River and attack Gloucester in the rear. My present strength will not admit of a detachment sufficient for this purpose without materially impairing the efficiency of this column." More definitely he writes to Secretary Stanton on the 10th: "The reconnaissance to-day, proves that it is necessary to invest and attack Gloucester Point. Give me Franklin's and McCall's divisions (of McDowell's corps), under command of Franklin, and I will at once undertake it. If circumstances of which I am not aware, make it impossible for you to send me two divisions to carry out this final plan of campaign, I will run the risk, and hold myself responsible for the results, if you will give me Franklin's division. If you still confide in my judgment, I entreat that you will grant this request. The fate of our cause depends upon it. Although willing, under the pressure of necessity, to carry this through with Franklin alone, I wish it to be distinctly understood that I think two divisions necessary. Franklin and his division are indispensable to me. General Barnard concurs in this view." And once more, on the 12th and 13th, he adds: "Franklin will attack on the other side. . . ." "Our work progressing well. We shall soon be at them, and I am sure of the result."

In response to these very urgent and confident expressions on McClellan's part, the President ordered Franklin's division to report to him forthwith; but it failed to reach the landing at Cheesman's Creek, below Yorktown, until the 20th of the month. Late as it was, preparations were begun to disembark the division on the Gloucester side, about three and a half miles below that point. A reconnaissance of the shore was made "a few days" after the arrival of the division by McClellan in person, in company with General Franklin, Captain Rodgers, of the navy, and Lieutenant-Colonel Alexander, of the Corps of Engineers. The latter officer was then instructed to devise the proper arrangements and superintend the landing of the troops; but, extraordinary as it may seem, more than two weeks were consumed in the preliminaries; and when everything was *nearly* ready for the disembarkation, the enemy had vanished from the scene! "All these preparations," to quote from Alexander's report, "were about completed, and we were engaged in making scaling-ladders, thinking we might be called upon to assault the works at Gloucester Point, when suddenly, on the morning of May 4th, the news spread through the fleet, that the enemy had evacuated Yorktown." How long it would have taken the whole of McDowell's corps to disembark at this rate, assuming that it was to disembark at the same point, the reader may judge; and yet for days it had been General McClellan's pet project, in connection with his plan of campaign, to utilize McDowell in just this manner as a flanking column. The merest novice in military matters would assume that every preparation for its prompt disembarkation would have been attended to, and delays avoided. So much for the project on the Gloucester side—excellent in conception, necessary to swift advance, but sadly interfered with by the Government; and, as far as attempted, too sluggishly prosecuted.

Surprised that he could not surround the place in the first instance, overawed by the appearance of the Warwick and its supposed defences, estimating the enemy's numbers far beyond the fact, and delayed or delaying in the attempt upon Gloucester—McClellan settled down to the scientific siege of Yorktown. Beyond noticing some of its incidents, we shall not dwell upon this final operation. It is clear that McClellan had it in contemplation, as an alternative, before he left Washington. Why take along a siege-train? If it was meant for the investment of Richmond, it should have come later by way of the James. It was out of place in active field movements. The Army of the Potomac had been placed in the General's hands as a drawn sword, to be wielded with rapid and sweeping effect; not only was success looked for, but immediate success. No wonder many hearts at the North betrayed anxiety, as time passed at Yorktown with nothing done and a siege in progress.

No doubt a brilliant siege operation would have been most acceptable to the country, as it certainly was coveted by McClellan, could it have been attended by the usual results of such an operation, namely, the capture of many prisoners, or the rout and demoralization of the enemy's force; but in this case, these results were not to be anticipated. There could be no siege in the true sense of the term. It was simply an approach to the enemy's position, which they could leave the moment they pleased, and in good order. Under the circumstances, it could hardly be regarded as a great triumph, that we were finally enabled to follow them.

Having determined thus to besiege Yorktown, McClellan appears to have given up all thought of piercing the Warwick line at any point; but meditated instead a grand assault on the main works after damaging them sufficiently with his heavy guns. The latter plan would have resulted in serious loss of life; with results less satisfactory, probably, than would have attended an attempt to break through at the weakest point. Reconnoissances, however, were made all along the front, and the enemy kept in anticipation of an attack; but no assaulting columns were ever organized, to take advantage of any opportunity offered. The brisk affair which occurred on April 16th, in front of Smith's division on the right of Keyes' corps, which has sometimes been represented as the beginning of a determined attack, had another purpose. "The object of the movement," says McClellan, "was to force the enemy to discontinue his work in strengthening his batteries, to silence his fire, and gain control of the dam existing at that point."*

* McClellan to Adjutant-General Thomas, April 19, 1862. This letter is not included in the former's official report.

The position in question was known as Dam No. 1, on the Warwick, nearly midway between Lee's and Wynn's Mills, and in front of a clearing just in advance of Smith's division, in which three burned chimneys stood—"Garrow's chimneys" the spot was called. On the rebel side, the crossing at the dam was covered by a one-gun battery; near which other works were supposed to be in process of construction. In pursuance of instructions conveyed by McClellan himself, General William F. Smith proceeded, on the morning of the 16th, to closely reconnoitre the position, and for the purpose, advanced Brooks' Vermont Brigade, with Captain Mott's Third New York Battery, toward the dam. The troops pushed well forward, carrying on a sharp fire; during which Smith examined the ground. "I ascertained from personal observation," he reports, "that the gun in the angle of the upper work had been replaced by a wooden gun, and that scarcely anybody showed above the parapet, the skirmishers from the Fourth Vermont doing good execution." More important was a daring feat on the part of Lieutenant E. M. Noyes, of the Third Vermont, aid to General Brooks, who actually crossed the Warwick below the dam, finding the water about waist-deep, and approached within fifty yards of the enemy's works undiscovered. Returning, he reported his observations to General McClellan, who now, about noon, had come upon the field, and who had ordered Smith to bring up his entire division to hold or command the advanced position occupied by Brooks' brigade. Smith, however, who heard what Lieutenant Noyes reported, went farther and obtained the consent of the General Commanding to push on a strong party across the stream, "to ascertain if the works had been sufficiently denuded to enable a column to effect a lodgement." Four companies of Colonel Hyde's Third Vermont, 200 strong, under

Captain F. C. Harrington, of that regiment, were accordingly ordered to advance and cross the Warwick, to determine, as Brooks reports, "the true state of affairs" on the other side. Promptly and gallantly the troops dashed through the water, and under a close fire from the enemy gained the latter's rifle-pits; which they held for over half an hour, returning the fire with spirit.

The enemy, who seem to have been surprised at this bold manœuvre, quickly increased in strength at this point. Magruder admits that the charge of the Vermonters was "very rapid and vigorous," and that the Fifteenth North Carolina, who were throwing up a work beyond the rifle-pits for the protection of their camp, were thrown into confusion and their Colonel, McKenney, killed in attempting to recover the pits. But other troops, including Anderson's Georgia brigade, under Howell Cobb, were brought up and the skirmish grew in intensity. Unfortunately, Captain Harrington failed to be reinforced in time; and receiving orders to withdraw, he recrossed the stream with a loss of 75 men, 22 of whom were killed. This was at about four o'clock in the afternoon.

The practicability of effecting a lodgement on the other side being thus demonstrated, another effort was made a little later; when four companies of the Sixth Vermont, under Colonel Lord, were ordered to cross at the point of Captain Harrington's advance, while Colonel Stoughton with four companies of the Fourth Vermont was directed to attempt the passage of the dam above, under the fire of the division batteries, all of which—20 guns—were brought into position. Lord's detachment, however, was met by a heavy fire from the now watchful enemy; and could not reach the rifle-pits. Colonel Stoughton reached the dam and prepared to push across, when General Smith ordered his return, and Lord followed. Notwithstanding the well-directed fire of the guns under Captain Ayres, Division Chief of Artillery, the enemy were able to deliver a heavy musketry fire; and the second attempt to cross was thus abandoned. "It will be apparent," says General Smith, in his report, "that no attempt to mass the troops of the division was made for an assault upon the works, but only such troops as were absolutely necessary to cover the movements of the companies of the Third and Fourth Vermont, and to be at hand to secure to us the enemy's works if we found them abandoned. The moment I found resistance serious, and the numbers opposed great, I acted in obedience to the *warning instructions* of the General-in-Chief, and withdrew the small number of troops exposed from under fire." Regret that the movement was not pushed is enhanced by Smith's reflection, that among the four companies of the Third Vermont, who first crossed the creek, there were "more individual acts of heroism performed" than he had ever before read of.

Thus a fair opportunity to break the Warwick line was missed. Had the same effort been made when the army first reached the line, there can be little doubt that success would have attended it.

Passing to the siege itself, we find that the operations were conducted with skill. Batteries were constructed under the supervision of Generals F. J. Porter, W. F. Barry, Chief of Artillery, and J. G. Barnard, Chief of Engineers; the former being designated as Director of the Siege. Nearly one hundred heavy Parrott guns, mortars, and howitzers were established opposite the town and the redoubts to its right, at ranges varying from fifteen hundred to two thousand yards. The enemy made but a slight effort to interfere with the work on our batteries and parallels; and on May 1st, Battery No. 1, on the bank of the river below the Moore House, was opened on the town and its dock, as Barnard reports, "with great effect." Four days later the fire was to open from all the guns and the siege pressed with vigor until the final assault should be deemed practicable.

There was at this time a small fleet of gunboats in the river (the greater part of the naval armament being still engaged at Hampton Roads watching the Merrimac), and their participation in the siege operations was expected, but how

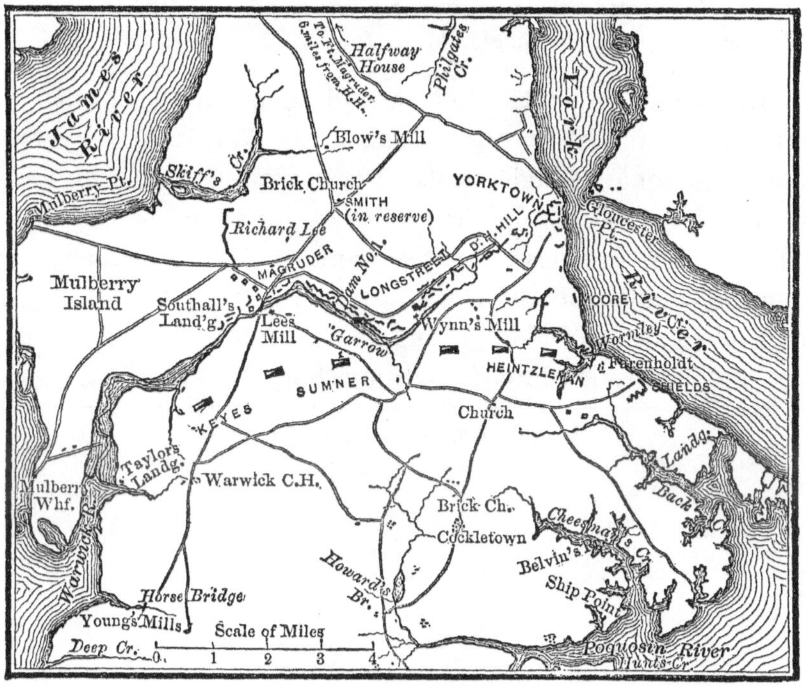

The Position at Yorktown.

much their officers felt able or willing to do may be gathered from the tenor of the following letter from Commander Missroon, of the Wachusett, to Admiral Goldsborough, dated April 23d:

"The works of the enemy are excessively strong and powerfully armed. Their cannon are managed and served with surprising accuracy, exceeding anything I have heretofore known, and there is every indication of a most determined resistance. More than fifty heavy cannon bear upon this bay, and the destruction of vessels of this class is inevitable, if taken under such a fire, without their having the power to inflict any damage, or but trifling damage to the enemy, owing to the superior and well-chosen position of their batteries. I believe that any number of vessels of this, or the gunboat class, will not prevail against works so located as those now before me, and that an increase of numbers will only add to our casualties. General McClellan proposes to dismount some of the cannon before these vessels advance, and it is an evident necessity that he should do so to a very large extent. . . . ."*

But the enemy were too shrewd to await our onslaught with guns and storming columns. By May 5th, they had remained long enough at the Yorktown line for their purpose. A month's time had been gained in keeping McClellan back, and early on the morning of the 5th, after an unusual cannonade of our lines during the previous night, they abandoned Yorktown and the Warwick line; retreating up the Peninsula through Williamsburg.

* From archives, Navy Department.

CHAPTER IV.

FORWARD FROM YORKTOWN — BATTLE OF WILLIAMSBURG.

THE evacuation of Yorktown took the Union army by surprise. If the somewhat tardy pursuit of the enemy be any indication, the movement was not anticipated at head-quarters. The troops had settled down to siege preparations, and a fixed camp life for at least a time longer. Hence, when orders came to break up and push after the rebels, several hours were consumed in having the commands properly provisioned for the march. The evacuation was reported at dawn, and the report confirmed soon after; it was not until noon that the cavalry and infantry were fairly off. The delay may have been immaterial; but it was a delay which presupposed the continuation of the siege.

The enemy, on their part, abandoned the place deliberately. If their retreat was a measure of safety, and so far forced upon them, it was still in accordance with a settled plan. They proposed to remain at the Warwick line only so long as prudence dictated, and for the single purpose of delaying McClellan. This they had succeeded in doing for an entire month. General Johnston is clear on this point. "It seemed to me," he reported May 19th, "that there were but two objects in remaining on the Peninsula. The possibility of an advance upon us by the enemy, and gaining time in which arms might be received and troops organized. I determined, therefore, to hold the position as long as it could be done without exposing our troops to the fire of the powerful artillery, which, I doubted not, would be brought to bear upon them. I believed that after silencing our batteries on York River, the enemy would attempt to turn us by moving up to West Point by water. . . . Circumstances indicating that the enemy's batteries were nearly ready, I directed the troops to move toward Williamsburg on the night of the 3d." His narrative on this point is to the same effect; in fact, Johnston, we have seen, did not favor the defence of the Peninsula, from the outset. On the 4th, at noon, his troops had all reached Williamsburg, whence they were ordered to march to Richmond, with Magruder's division leading.

The Union forces, once upon the road, hurried after the retreating enemy. Stoneman, with the cavalry, received orders to harass their rear, and, if possible, cut off that portion of it which must have taken the longer route by the Lee's Mills road. As the rebels had some twelve hours the start—the rear, certainly six—Stoneman could not have accomplished the latter object. He caught up with Stuart's cavalry near the Half-way House, which fell back skirmishing as far as a line of redoubts which Magruder had thrown up long before as a possible defensive position across the Peninsula—the most westerly of the three he had partially or wholly completed. When Stoneman neared this line, of which he had but a vague, if any knowledge, he sent General Emory to the left, to head off such rebels as might be on that road. Emory encountered a cavalry regiment and battery under Stuart himself; but, without infantry supports, could not corner them. To the front, Stoneman pursued with General Cooke's command of the First and Sixth Regular Cavalry, and a battery of horse-artillery; and soon encountered the works referred to. The larger redoubt, in his immediate front, Fort Magruder, was occupied, while those to its left seemed to be empty; but as he manœuvred and skirmished, the enemy were seen to be reoccupying them, and he retired to await the arrival of infantry. In doing so, the enemy attacked him, though without much effect; the one piece of artillery that was lost had to be abandoned in the mud, after the unavailing efforts of ten horses to bring it off.

To follow and co-operate with Stoneman, the infantry divisions of Hooker, of the Third Corps, and Smith of the Fourth, were directed by McClellan, to take the lead of the columns and hasten forward—Hooker marching by the direct and shorter road on the right from Yorktown to Williamsburg, and Smith filing from his position opposite "Dam No. 1," into the Lee's Mills road on the left. Kearney was to follow Hooker; Couch and Casey were to follow Smith. In the afternoon of the next day, the divisions of Sedgwick and Richardson, or Sumner's corps, were also set in motion, while Franklin and Porter remained at Yorktown to go up the river in transports. The entire army was thus upon its feet again, with the eyes of the country intent upon its progress.

The General Commanding, not anticipating any serious engagement during the first day or two of the pursuit, kept his headquarters near Yorktown, to superintend what he regarded as the more important advance of Franklin by water. The direction of the divisions moving by land, was accordingly assigned to Sumner, second in rank to the Chief. His instructions, received at noon on the 4th, were "to take command of the troops ordered in pursuit of the enemy" until McClellan's arrival. General Heintzelman, on the other hand, moving with his corps, confesses some surprise at finding Sumner at the front and in charge, since he reports that he had been directed "to take control of the entire movement" himself. It is probable that Heintzelman was expected to be in the advance sooner than Sumner, where his "control," until the latter's arrival, would be necessary. As it was, they seemed, with Keyes, the remaining corps commander, to act in unison during the approaching events; but the tone of certain passages in Heintzelman's report and the sensitive reply of Sumner, indicate, that as between these two officers, an undercurrent of jealousy or unfriendliness existed, which, on a subsequent occasion, came near working mischief.

The troops under Sumner's command, who were to become identified more than others with the approaching battle of Williamsburg, were Hooker's, Smith's, Kearney's and part of Couch's divisions. Hooker on the march was expected to be up first to support the cavalry. Smith, moving on the parallel road to the left, made greater progress, but was stopped at the head of Skiff Creek, by the burning of the bridge. Between two and three o'clock, Sumner ordered him to turn to the right and into the road which Hooker was following. Smith reached it near the Half-way house just before Hooker's troops came up; and keeping on, obliged the latter to halt for over three hours. Contrary, thus, to the original intention, Smith was in the same road with, and in advance of Hooker, scarcely six miles distant from their respective starting-points; and as Hooker now could not act as the immediate support of the cavalry, he suggested to his Corps Commander, Heintzelman, who consented, that after advancing about three miles, he in turn should cross over to the road Smith was to have followed, and where Emory's cavalry were, and pursue or attack from that direction. How far this apparent confusion and change of place on the part of the two divisions affected the pursuit on that day may be a question, Stoneman claiming that had Smith been able to continue on the Lee's Mills road he might have assisted Emory and his cavalry in capturing Stuart's troopers; while Hooker, with his own road clear before him, could have pushed on and taken possession of the enemy's works before they could be reoccupied. But, as a matter of fact, Stuart was in no immediate danger; and as to the works, Smith reached the front, under Sumner, quite as soon as Hooker could have done.

Smith's division—Hancock's brigade in advance—came up with the cavalry about half-past five o'clock in the afternoon. Sumner, who tells us that he felt "the importance of pressing the pursuit as fast as possible," encouraged by Stoneman's representations, that the infantry could accomplish what the cavalry could not, determined, late as it was, to advance at once upon the enemy. Forming his division in three lines of battle, Smith prepared for a charge through a piece of woods and beyond to the works. It was half-past six before the lines moved; and hardly did they move before the woods were found to be "utterly impracticable." What with the close, tangled undergrowth and the increasing darkness in which the formations could not be preserved, a halt was ordered and the troops bivouacked where they were, Sumner, himself, did not join Hancock and Brooks until dawn; whence the report arose, that he had lost his way and slept at the foot of a tree between our own and the enemy's pickets.* Hooker, meanwhile,after filing to the left, marched until eleven o'clock at night, halting at about the same distance from the enemy that Smith was, on the main road to his right.

On the following morning the battle of Williamsburg opened,—a battle fought without a plan, with inadequate numbers, and at a serious sacrifice without compensating re-

* Letter of Colonel C. S. Stuart, U. S. Eng.

sult. The responsibility has been laid by some upon the shoulders of McClellan because of his absence from the field; and by others upon Sumner, who seems to have directed the movements of the day without method. Whatever may have prevented McClellan's presence with the advance, one might at least expect that his senior corps commander should have been competent to fight a battle of moderate proportions.

Hooker began the attack. He began it on the strength of the orders he had received from McClellan the previous morning, before leaving Yorktown—a noteworthy feature of the battle, in view of the fact that three corps commanders, Sumner, Heintzelman, and Keyes, were then at the front, and the former in command. Heintzelman, to whose corps Hooker belonged, thought, as we infer from his report, that Sumner should have given directions to the leading divisions on the preceding night, if a battle was imminent, and states that he could not be found; but he nevertheless failed himself to caution Hooker as to his movements, without first hearing from Sumner. So Hooker, in the position of an independent commander, moved to attack the enemy early on the morning of the 5th. There was something vigorous about his action. Despite the rain which was falling plentifully, and the thick, slippery mud, into which the artillery wheels sank deep, he pressed forward and soon became engaged. Fort Magruder stood in his immediate front commanding the junction of the left or Hampton road, into which he had turned, and the main Yorktown road, where Sumner, with Smith's division, was to be found. To the right and left the smaller redoubts, twelve in all, formed an irregular line nearly across the peninsula. Resting on creeks and marshes, with a belt of clearing in their front, they could have proved, if properly manned and supported, a formidable barrier. The approaches to the line were singularly disadvantageous for the attacking party, thick woods lining the roads, in which artillery could not operate, and the clearings being "dotted all over," as Hooker reports, with rifle-pits, from which a deadly fire was directed against the troops while taking up position.

As early as half-past seven, the First Brigade, Grover's, was at work. "Being in pursuit of a retreating army," says Hooker, "I deemed it my duty to lose no time in making the disposition of my forces to attack, regardless of their number and position, except to accomplish the result with the least possible sacrifice of life. By so doing, my division, if it did not capture the army before me, would at least hold it that some others might . . . . and Grover was directed to commence the attack." The latter opened fire upon the rifle-pits from the woods to the right and left of the road, and Webber's and Bramhall's batteries were brought into action on the right, some seven hundred yards from Fort Magruder. By nine o'clock the fort was silenced and all the enemy's troops in sight on the plain dispersed. This was satisfactory, as well as the movement of two of Grover's regiments on the right, who were directed by Hooker to open up communication with Sumner on the Yorktown road. These regiments, the Eleventh Massachusetts and Twenty-sixth Pennsylvania, skirmished through the woods, found no enemy, communicated with Sumner's command, and the former returning, reported the fact to Hooker, who now felt that he was not fighting in an isolated position, but on the left of a general line which could be kept connected under the control of his superior.

Meanwhile, the rear divisions of the enemy had halted in their retreat. The demonstration of the Union cavalry the previous afternoon, and Hooker's pressure early the next morning, compelled them to face about to escape being run over at will by their pursuers. Johnston left Longstreet in command at Williamsburg, on the 5th, and that officer, in the course of the morning, put his entire division in front of Hooker. As the successive brigades went into action, it increased in intensity, and, at eleven o'clock, Hooker found himself warmly engaged. R. H. Anderson's and Pryor's brigades formed the right and left of the enemy's line. Wilcox reinforced Anderson, with A. P. Hill in supporting distance, and, at ten o'clock, Pickett's brigade was also added. These brigades Longstreet directed against Hooker's centre and left, and endeavored to turn his position. They issued from and about the redoubts to the right of Fort Magruder into a wooded ravine, and pressed in masses upon our line. The left especially was in danger, where Patterson's Third Brigade, of New Jersey troops, was fighting manfully against superior numbers. Grover, who also felt the attack, moved part of his first brigade to Patterson's support. The line nevertheless was pushed back as far as the batteries in the road, and that of Webber was lost, and Bramhall's abandoned but recovered again. The situation was growing serious, and Hooker called for reinforcements, or rather for a diversion in his favor. At half-past eleven he sent a note to Heintzelman, who was supposed to be with Sumner. "I have had a hard contest all the morning," he wrote, "but do not despair of success. My men are hard at work, but a good deal exhausted. It is reported to me that my communication with you by the Yorktown road is clear of the enemy. Batteries, cavalry, and infantry can take post by the side of mine to whip the enemy." It was this latter suggestion that should have been followed out, but Heintzelman was not in command and did not receive the message, as he had started by a roundabout road to reach Hooker, and

Sumner, to whom the note was handed, returned it with the single endorsement that he had opened and read it. Just before that he had sent word to Kearney to hurry to Hooker's support. Why he did not send Casey, who was much nearer, and two of whose brigades were once ordered to Hooker and then ordered back, is not perfectly clear. There was confusion in the instructions.

Thus from seven o'clock, A.M., till about twelve, Hooker, alone on the left, had been doing all the fighting. No troops fell into line of battle on his right. No other line was engaged anywhere during the forenoon.

This state of things reveals the true defect of the Williamsburg affair. The fact is that when Hooker began his attack, Sumner, Heintzelman, and Keyes had adopted another plan of action, irrespective of Hooker. There was no concerted movement; hence failure.

The plan these corps commanders agreed upon at an informal consultation early in the morning meditated a flank movement around the enemy's left. Neither of them seemed to know what Hooker proposed to do. They looked to another part of the field. A countryman had reported that the rebels had not occupied certain works on their left, and negroes, questioned by Keyes and others, confirmed the story. To put the matter beyond doubt, Captain Stewart, of the Engineer Corps, and four companies of the Fourth Vermont, were sent, under General Smith's direction, to ascertain the topography of the country, and learn whether a road existed by which the works in question could be seized or turned, if found to be occupied. At ten o'clock Stewart reported that a redoubt, covering a stream called Cub Dam Creek, on the right, seemed to be abandoned. Sumner then directed General Hancock, who was sent for, to march with his own and part of Davidson's brigades, of Smith's division, and Cowan's New York Battery, of six guns, and take the redoubt.

The passage of the dam was only practicable by the narrow mill bridge across its breast, and which was about two hundred and thirty feet in length. The Fifth Wisconsin and Sixth Maine in column of assault, Major Larrabee commanding the skirmishers, entered the redoubt and found it unoccupied.* Hancock immediately garrisoned it with three companies of the Thirty-third New York, as a rear guard. He then threw his skirmishers into the open field beyond the earthwork, the remainder of his infantry in line of battle to their rear, with the artillery in the centre. At twelve o'clock, word was dispatched to Smith that the redoubt and the important position at Cub Dam Creek were in possession of the Union troops, under Hancock. Here was the first advantage gained by the Federals, and it ultimately determined the result. By this time Hooker's entire command had been precipitated against the enemy on the left. This stubborn fight so engrossed the attention of the Confederate leader that Hancock's manœuvre had been executed before its dangerous significance became apparent. But Hancock was uneasy and readily appreciated the necessity of securing another work, two-thirds of a mile in advance, as it commanded the position he then occupied. He accordingly requested Smith to reinforce him with a brigade of infantry to protect his rear from sudden assault.

Smith promised him four regiments and one battery. Acting on this assurance Hancock took quiet possession of the advance redoubt. In order to divert the heavy firing on Hooker, he (Hancock) now determined to engage the enemy and endeavor to drive them out of two works nearest to his front. His position was a strong one, having a crest

* Lieutenant Custer, the late cavalry general, led the way. See General Hancock's Report, p. 730, War Records.

and natural glacis on either flank, extending to the woods on the right and left. Advancing his skirmishers he soon drove the enemy out of the position, but declined occupying it, as the reinforcements did not arrive. A little later he deemed it prudent to fall back to a crest near the redoubt first reached.

By these movements on our right, the enemy were forced to pay special attention to Hancock. They proposed to attack him. Johnston states that neither he nor Longstreet knew of the abandoned redoubts until late in the afternoon, when General Early sent an officer to report the situation in that part of the field, and request permission to drive off the Union troops, which Johnston gave. D. H. Hill, senior in command on that flank, was directed to take charge of the movement. Four regiments were pushed forward. Early led the Twenty-fourth and Thirty-eighth Virginia on the left; Hill commanded the Fifth and Twenty-third North Carolina on the right. They crossed a stream in their front, and pushed through a dense undergrowth to an open field. In this passage the line was broken, and when the brigade reached the open, the left wing was in advance, chasing the "Yankees," according to Hill, who soon found himself in a most unpleasant position. For, as the rebels emerged into easy range, Hancock, who appeared to be retiring, turned upon them—his men cheering and firing over the crest mentioned—and dealt destruction in their ranks. The volleys of musketry were followed up with an effective charge. Early was wounded and many of his men and officers fell. Hill endeavored to support him, but his regiments could not be handled under fire, and the entire force fell back. It had suffered a bloody repulse, losing nearly 400 men. Hill's and Early's discomfited commands remained in line of battle at a distance all night, expecting to be attacked, and suffered greatly from the cold rain that fell.

This conduct of Hancock and his command was the relieving feature of the day. "The brilliancy of the plan of battle," reports General Smith, "the coolness of its execution, the seizing of the proper instant for changing from the defensive to the offensive, the steadiness of the troops engaged, and the completeness of the victory, are subjects to which I earnestly call the attention of the General-in-Chief for his just praise."

Upon the left, meantime, Hooker had been fighting manfully, but lost ground, until Kearney came to his relief about two o'clock, and threw Birney's and Berry's brigades into the action, with Jameson's forming a second line. Hooker's men fell back out of fire, exhausted and with thinned ranks. Kearney engaged the enemy vigorously, and by nightfall had recovered the field. About the same time in the afternoon, two o'clock, Couch's division appeared on the ground on the main road, and Peck's brigade was ordered to deploy as near as possible on Hooker's right, where he also became closely engaged, but held his own. When night closed, the Union forces were still confronting the line of rebel works. The tactics of the day had proved a failure. Sumner had hoped to accomplish something by Hancock's move, but was distracted by Hooker's serious action. He proposed to reinforce Hancock with the rest of Smith's division, but the heavy firing on his left warned him that the enemy might succeed in interposing themselves between Hooker and Smith, and the latter was retained near the centre, or rather near the main road; for it would be within the truth to say that up to two o'clock, when Peck arrived, there was no centre to this battle. During the forenoon at least, Hooker was fighting a battle of his own on the left and Sumner was planning to fight another on the right. At the moment the latter wished to follow up his own plan and push

Hancock forward, Hooker's somewhat alarming situation, which had not been counted on, suddenly baffled him. In a word, neither Sumner nor any one else had the entire field under his eye and control. The battle was fought by piecemeal and ended in disappointment. We lost that day, 2,228 killed, wounded, and missing, and five guns. Longstreet reports the total rebel loss at 1,560.

Toward five o'clock the continued cheering of troops at Sumner's front announced the arrival of General McClellan upon the field. He had hastily ridden forward on receiving the tardy intelligence, conveyed to him by two members of his staff, that matters were not going on well at the front. There he made the necessary dispositions for more united action on the following day. By this time the divisions of Hooker, Kearney, Smith, Couch, and Casey were well in hand. Sedgwick's and Richardson's were turned back to Yorktown to follow Franklin's and Porter's to West Point by water.

At night the enemy abandoned Williamsburg, and continued their retreat toward Richmond.

That portion of the army that was to advance by water from Yorktown made more comfortable progress and at less sacrifice than the divisions which had been marching by land and fighting at Williamsburg. Something more was expected of it at first than simple progress. It was intended that Franklin, followed by Porter, Sedgwick, and Richardson, should be moved in transports to West Point above, and striking across to the main roads, cut off the retreat of such bodies of the enemy as might be below. But delays, as usual, prevented. Franklin, whose troops had been so long on the boats, tiring of inaction, obtained permission the day before the evacuation of Yorktown to land his men and go into camp. Ordered back again the next day, it was evening before all were ready to steam forward, and then, in consequence of the extreme darkness of the night, the commander of the gunboat flotilla declined to act as convoy until the following morning. So Franklin did not get off from Yorktown until the 6th. At one o'clock he reached Eltham Landing above West Point, disembarked his troops, and immediately sent the transports back for Sedgwick's division. His instructions were to wait at Eltham until further orders. No mention was made about cutting off the enemy. To make the attempt alone would have been hazardous, and the remaining divisions could not concentrate for several days. Franklin, indeed, on the 7th, was himself attacked. About nine o'clock in the morning, a large force of the enemy appeared in front of General Newton's brigade, which they attacked with vigor an hour later. Parts of Slocum's and Taylor's brigades supported Newton, and a smart action continued until three o'clock, when the enemy withdrew. Their object in attacking was twofold: first, to protect their trains, which were in an exposed position at Barhamsville, and upon which they apprehended an assault from the troops landed from the transports at West Point; and second to drive the Union army into the river if they could, or, at least, send them back under the protection of their gunboats. The rebel force consisted of Whiting's division of G. W. Smith's command, the command of General Magruder, then under Brigadier-General Jones, and Hill and Longstreet's forces in reserve.

CHAPTER V.

TO THE CHICKAHOMINY — McDOWELL — JACKSON IN THE SHENANDOAH VALLEY — AFFAIR OF HANOVER COURT HOUSE.

AFTER Williamsburg, as from the outset, the course of advance up the peninsula lay straight toward Richmond, with the base of supplies either on the York or the James. The York was followed, and within two weeks the army had again been concentrated, resting between that river, or its southern branch—the Pamunkey—and the Chickahominy. From Williamsburg, the distance marched in the interval was no more than forty miles—the few and wretched roads continuing to prove serious obstacles—and the promise of a rapid pursuit failed of being made good. The troops moved on the 8th, Keyes in advance, following Stoneman's cavalry, who opened communication with Franklin at Eltham. On the 15th, headquarters were established at Cumberland on the south bank of the Pamunkey, and on the following day at the White House, where a permanent depot was organized, the troops having marched up through Barhamsville, Roper's Church, and New Kent Court House. On the 21st the army was collected and in line once more, with its face toward Richmond, from seven to twelve miles distant. The intervening obstacles to be overcome were the ever-present enemy, and in addition, as it was to prove, the formidable Chickahominy. Porter's newly organized corps* held the right of the line three miles from New Bridge, with Franklin's corps, also just formed, supporting, while Sumner occupied the centre, connecting with Keyes, who held the left near Bottom's Bridge, with Heintzelman in reserve. Stoneman and the cavalry watched the extreme right within a mile of New Bridge.

The position thus occupied by the Union army is one to be noticed, since General McClellan implies in his report that it was not entirely his own choice. The reason of his being there, as explained by himself, introduces the reader to a new phase of the campaign, with McDowell reappearing as the aid with whom alone success could be hoped for.

Soon after the Williamsburg battle McClellan resumed his calls for a larger force. Casualties and sickness had reduced his numbers considerably, and on the 14th he reported that he could not put into battle against the enemy more than 80,000 men at the utmost. Johnston, he believed, was far stronger. To the President he reported: "I have found no fighting men left in this Peninsula. All are in the ranks of the opposing foe;" and then he urged that he might be reinforced with all the disposable troops of the Government. "I ask for every man that the War Department can send me," was his powerful appeal. "I will fight the enemy," he continues, "whatever their force may be, with whatever force I may have, and I firmly believe that we shall beat them, but our triumph should be made decisive and complete. The soldiers of this army love their Government,

---

* The two new "Provisional" Corps, as they were called, became the Fifth and Sixth. They were organized about May 15th, by making Franklin commander of the latter, which was composed of his own division, now Slocum's, with Smith's from Keyes' Corps, and Fitz John Porter commander of the former, including his own division, now Morell's, and another under Sykes. The latter's brigade of regulars had been enlarged to a division by the addition of Duryea's New York Zouaves, and the Tenth New York, under Colonel Bendix.

and will fight well in its support. You may rely upon them. They have confidence in me as their General, and in you as their President. Strong reinforcements will at least save the lives of many of them. The greater our force the more perfect will be our combinations, and the less our loss."

To this pressing entreaty for more troops, President Lincoln returned an encouraging reply. There was McDowell's corps, which had been withheld from the Peninsula Army since March, still in front of Washington. It had been guarding the city with eminent satisfaction during McClellan's weary progress toward Richmond, and was to continue there for that purpose until the Government could safely spare it for more active operations. "You will consider the national capital," wrote Stanton to McDowell, April 11th, "as especially under your protection, and make no movement throwing your force out of position for the discharge of this primary duty." McDowell repaired first to Catlett's Station, and in the direction of Culpeper, and soon after moved down the Rappahannock opposite to Fredericksburg, intending to occupy that town as his advanced defensive position in front of Washington. To supply the place of Franklin's division of his corps which had joined McClellan, General Shields' division of Banks' Shenandoah force was ordered to report to him. With his corps thus augmented and completed—his four Division Commanders being McCall, King, Ord, and Shields—General McDowell could muster, about May 20th, the very respectable army of 41,000 men, inclusive of a brigade of cavalry and 100 pieces of artillery. Opposed to him, hovering to the south of and in the vicinity of Fredericksburg, was a fluctuating force of the rebels, generally some twelve thousand strong, commanded by Brigadier-General J. R. Anderson, of the Tredegar Iron Works, Virginia.

It was necessarily to McDowell's command that President Lincoln looked when he received McClellan's urgent call for reinforcements. There were no other troops to be had. On May 17th, accordingly, the former received instructions to move down the Richmond and Fredericksburg Railroad and "co-operate" with the army under McClellan, then threatening the Confederate capital, as we have seen, from the line of the Pamunkey and York Rivers. It will be observed that this was not a reinforcement proper, but an independent co-operating army. The "primary duty" of protecting Washington still outweighed all other considerations, and McDowell thus could not, in the eyes of the Government, be placed under the untrammelled command of McClellan with any more reason now than at the beginning of the campaign. Stanton's reply to the latter presents the situation perfectly. "Your despatch to the President," he writes, May 17th, 2 P.M., "asking reinforcements, has been received and carefully considered. The President is not willing to uncover the capital entirely, and it is believed that, even if this were prudent, it would require more time to effect a junction between your army and that of the Rappahannock by the way of the Potomac and York rivers than by a land march. In order, therefore, to increase the strength of the attack upon Richmond at the earliest moment, General McDowell has been ordered to march upon that city by the shortest route. . . . At your earnest call for reinforcements he is sent forward to co-operate in the reduction of Richmond, but charged, in attempting this, not to uncover the city of Washington; and you will give no orders, either before or after your junction, which can put him out of position to cover this city."

To these instructions McClellan demurred at the time only so far as to request that McDowell be placed under his orders in the usual way after the junction, and the obligation imposed upon himself not to uncover Washington; and to this the President assented. What seems strange, however, in the perusal of the despatches, is that McClellan felt hampered rather than relieved by the Government's answer to his appeal. The claim, for instance, is made in that document that the order to McDowell to move down upon Richmond forced him to take up a position to the north of that city and establish depots on the Pamunkey, by which he was prevented from using the James River as a line of operations. "I had advised and preferred," writes the General, "that reinforcements should be sent by water for the reasons that their arrival would be more safe and certain, and that I would be left free to rest the army on the James River whenever the navigation of that stream should be opened. . . . Had General McDowell joined me by water I could have approached Richmond by the James, and thus avoided the delays and losses incurred in bridging the Chickahominy, and would have had the army massed in one body instead of being necessarily divided by that stream." But in regard to this, it is but repeating the proper criticisms made by other writers that General McClellan had frequently mentioned the Pamunkey as his prospective base, that he made no representation to the Government at the time that he wished to be free to move by the James, and that (to anticipate somewhat) it was within his power during the first three weeks of June, when he found that McDowell was again withheld from him, to follow the latter route. On one point there can be no question, that the position of his army, as already given, along the left bank of the Chickahominy from Bottom's toward New Bridge, on May 20th, with the White House, on the Pamunkey, as the base of supplies, was one of McClellan's own choice, uninfluenced by McDowell's movements.

The interests of the North and the reputations of the generals commanding everywhere in the field called loudly for action and success. It was time something was done, especially in Virginia. Forty thousand or even twenty thousand men joined to McClellan's army would seem to have made it irresistible, regardless of the route it might take. McClellan must have thought so then, whatever he may have written afterward, and it is certain that he did his part to form a junction with McDowell as soon as possible. Unfortunately for the fate of the campaign the latter was delayed. It was ten days after the order to move down, before he could do so. That delay, at least, could not be laid at McClellan's doors. Shield's division for one thing was behind in its supplies, but could not the other three have advanced without him? The very demonstration might have proved effectual in preventing or modifying the subsequent situation in the Shenandoah Valley, which so seriously disturbed the situation on the Peninsula. Not until the 26th could McDowell promise to march.

But McDowell was destined not to move toward Richmond at all. The fatality which had so far attended the Peninsula movements, was to afflict other fields nearer Washington. A new element had now to be considered in calculating the chances of the campaign—"Stonewall" Jackson; and to the field of his fame, the Shenandoah Valley, let us turn for a moment.

In December, 1861, Rosecrans, who commanded in West Virginia, proposed to occupy Winchester, as the best way to cover that State, and guard the Baltimore and Ohio Railway. His plan was foiled by Jackson, who took possession of Winchester in force, in November of that year. In January, 1862, he moved against Bath, in Morgan County, which was evacuated; but General Lander, who had succeeded

Rosecrans in command, prevented him from crossing the Potomac—though not from damaging the railroad and placing himself between General Lander at Hancock, and Kelly at Romney. Compelling the evacuation of Romney, Jackson remained in winter quarters at Winchester, until the advance of Banks, in March, obliged him to withdraw to Woodstock, forty miles farther south. As soon as this advance of Banks relieved McClellan of anxiety as to that quarter, he ordered Banks, on March 16th, to post his command in the vicinity of Manassas, to rebuild the railway from Washington, occupy Winchester, and scour the country south of the railroad and up the Shenandoah Valley. Shields was withdrawn from Strasburg, and Jackson immediately followed him. Ashby's cavalry came up with his rear guard within a mile of Winchester—and encamped for the night at Kernstown, three miles south of that place, where he was joined by Jackson with his whole force at 2 P.M. on March 23d. Shields, who did not expect an attack, had posted his force on a ridge near Kernstown, with Kimball's brigade and Daum's artillery in advance, Sullivan's in his rear, and Tyler with Broadhead's cavalry in reserve. Jackson, who was deceived as to the number of the troops in his front, attacked about three o'clock, and led his men, weary as they were by a long march, against the ridge where the right flank of Shields was posted, hoping to turn it and cut them off from Winchester. The impetus of his assault was sufficient to carry him to the top of the ridge, but there Shields held him until he brought his own reserves into action and became the attacking party.

After a stubborn contest of three hours, Jackson was defeated, with the loss of two guns and 200 prisoners, besides 500 killed and wounded. The unexpected audacity of this attack had immediate and important results; Banks' corps was turned back from its march to the Potomac and Manassas, and he himself returned to take command of the pursuit, which was continued to Woodstock. A few days later, March 31st, Blenker's division, 10,000 strong, was ordered to join Fremont, lately appointed to the command in West Virginia—with instructions to report to Banks, and remain with him as long as there was any apprehension of Jackson's renewing the attack. Banks followed Jackson up the valley, and about April 20th, the latter took up a strong position at Swift Run gap—his front covered by the Shenandoah, his flanks by the mountains, and with good roads to his rear, toward Gordonsville, where lay General Ewell's division of Johnston's army, within easy reach. Should Banks endeavor to go on to Staunton, he exposed his flank and rear and his line of communication with the Potomac to attack from Jackson, while if he attacked Jackson, and should be defeated, his army would be cut off in the heart of a hostile country.

This was the situation on April 28th, when Jackson again assumed the offensive, and began that succession of movements which ended in the complete derangement of the Union plans in Virginia—on the Peninsula as well as in the Shenandoah.

In order that he might operate effectively, Jackson applied to Lee for reinforcements, and asked that Ewell's division might be given him. Lee answered on the 29th, that he feared to detach Ewell, lest he should invite an attack on Richmond and peril the safety of the army on the Peninsula; but he put the command of Edward Johnson, 3,500 strong, then at West View, seven miles west of Staunton, under his orders. The letter suggests that in case Jackson should feel strong enough to hold Banks in check, Ewell and Anderson's army near Fredericksburg might attack McDowell between that place and Acquia Creek, with much promise of success. This shows that the great flank movement of Jackson, made later, was not then thought of.

At that time the Union forces in Northern Virginia were disposed as follows: Banks with about 20,000 men near Harrisonburg; Schenck and Milroy, of Fremont's corps, with 6,000 men, had pushed their pickets east of the mountains and were in front of Johnson; Fremont, with 10,000 more, was marching to join them; McDowell, with 40,000, was at Fredericksburg. Jackson proceeded to act. Joining his own forces and Johnson's he moved promptly to attack Milroy, leaving Ewell, who was freed by McDowell's change of position, to watch Banks. Jackson moved by a roundabout course to Staunton. Pushing forward from that place, he reached the village of McDowell, where he gained a hill which commanded the camps of Milroy and Schenck, who had united. These, in order to escape, were obliged to attack Jackson in his strong position on Sittlington's Hill. The battle continued for three or four hours, but was unfavorable to the Union arms. Their forces were withdrawn during the night and retired to Franklin, where a junction was made with Fremont. Banks' force had been weakened by Shields' division sent to McDowell, and learning that Ewell was in the valley, he fell back to New Market, and thence to Strasburg, which he fortified to cover the valley and the Baltimore and Ohio Railroad. Jackson followed swiftly, united with Ewell, and fell upon Colonel Eenly's force of 1,000 men at Front Royal, which he destroyed, and thence pressed forward against Banks, who, hearing of his approach, retreated in considerable confusion and disorder to Winchester. Here he made a stand, but the rebel attack was too vigorous and in too overwhelming numbers to be resisted. The retreat was resumed and did not stop short of the Potomac River.

The sudden intelligence of Banks' reverses, and the fact that Jackson was on the Potomac, caused the wildest excitement at Washington. McDowell, who had already taken up his line of march to join McClellan, was turned back and ordered to put 20,000 men in motion at once for the Shenandoah, in conjunction with Fremont, to capture the force of Jackson and Ewell; and on the 24th McClellan was advised by telegraph from the President that he must not look for co-operation from that quarter. So here again did the promising plan on the Peninsula fall through. McClellan was not to have McDowell's 40,000 men. Both generals protested or represented to the Government that Jackson's movement was evidently intended as a "scare," and that not only was Washington not in danger, but that an attempt to entrap "Stonewall" in the Valley by moving part of McDowell's corps to that quarter would probably not succeed. The Government authorities and "advisers" however, appear to have been in no mood to listen to calm military reasoning, and McDowell was again withheld from McClellan, while his reinforcements, as predicted, could effect nothing against Jackson. The latter eluded Fremont, approaching from the West, and Shields' from the East, fought and gained the battles of Cross Keys and Port Republic, and resumed a safe position up the Valley. By these flying movements he had paralyzed McDowell's force, which was to have, and should have, joined McClellan and fallen like a hammer upon Richmond.*

---

* The proceedings of the McDowell Court of Inquiry in December, 1862, contain important testimony and documents in regard to this period of the campaign. The following is a brief extract from General McClellan's statements:

"I have no doubt said, for it has ever been my opinion, that the Army of the Potomac would have taken Richmond had not the corps of General McDowell been separated from it. It is also my opinion that had the command of General McDowell joined the Army of the Potomac in the month of May by way of Han-

Proceeding with the narrative of McClellan's movements, we recall the fact that Anderson's rebel brigade was near Fredericksburg, and a part of Stewart's cavalry also, watching the movements of McDowell. Branch's brigade was at Hanover Court House, fourteen miles north of Richmond. The two brigades, in number some twelve thousand men, thus interposed between the right of McClellan and McDowell's line of advance, was a threat which was not to be disregarded. They were at once a menace to his flank and McDowell's approach. When McClellan was advised of these facts, and that McDowell's forward movement had begun, he resolved to take the initiative and strike a blow at Branch which should make him harmless for a time, relieve his own flank and rear, hinder him from reinforcing Jackson and impeding McDowell, who at this time was eight miles south of Fredericksburg.

This task was intrusted to General Fitz John Porter with a command of his own selection, about 12,000 strong. Porter adds that the object of the expedition was "to clear the enemy from the Upper Peninsula as far as Hanover Court House or beyond;" the destruction of the bridges over the South Anna and Pamunkey Rivers, in order to prevent the enemy in large force from getting into our rear from that direction, and in order, further, to cut one great line of the enemy's communications, *i.e.,* that "connecting Richmond directly with Northern Virginia."

For the destruction of the bridges over the Pamunkey, Warren's brigade had been already detailed and had been posted at Old Church. It was composed, provisionally, of the Fifth New York, Warren's regiment, the Thirteenth New

---

over Court House from Fredericksburg, that we would have had Richmond within a week after the junction. I do not hold General McDowell responsible in my own mind for the failure to join me on either occasion."

York, under Colonel Marshall, the First Connecticut Artillery under Colonel R. O. Tyler, the Sixth Pennsylvania Cavalry and Weeden's battery. This force had already been successful in destroying all means of communication over the Pamunkey as far as Hanover Court House. On the morning of May 27th the brigade moved toward the Court House, on a road running parallel to the Pamunkey. At 4 A.M. the same day General Porter left New Bridge with General Morell's division, consisting of his old brigade, commanded by Colonel McQuade, and Generals Butterfield's and Martindale's brigades. This infantry force was preceded by an advance guard under General Emory, composed of the Fifth and Sixth regiments of United States Cavalry and Benson's Horse Battery of the Second United States Artillery. The route was from New Bridge, via Mechanicsville, to Hanover Court House, north.

As usual, it rained heavily and the roads were reduced to a terrible condition. About noon, the cavalry, upon passing the junction of the Ashland road and the Hanover Court House road, encountered a portion of Branch's brigade of North Carolina men, which, supporting two pieces of artillery posted near Dr. Kinney's house, attempted to hold the road leading to the Court House. Colonel Johnson's regiment, the Twenty-fifth New York Volunteers, was moving with the cavalry, with skirmishers deployed, and came in direct collision with a portion of Branch's command, which extended into the woods on the right and east of the Court House road. The cavalry had disengaged itself from the main column and had moved toward the front, leaving Benson's battery engaged with the rebels, who had developed at that time but little strength. Owing to our ignorance of the enemy's position, a portion of Johnson's regiment was captured near Kinney's house, by that portion of the enemy which had been passed by the cavalry, and which was hidden by the woods before alluded to. One piece of rebel artillery was driven from the field and one piece disabled by Benson. Upon reaching the front General Porter, finding that the existence of both infantry and artillery had been developed during this action near Kinney's house, deployed General Butterfield's brigade in two lines and directed him to charge and drive the rebels from the wheat field. Butterfield's brigade moved over in handsome style, as if on parade, captured the gun and cleared the field. It was then supposed that the enemy had retreated from his front in the direction of Hanover Court House, and orders were given to pursue. But upon approaching the junction of these roads, General Porter sent toward Ashland two regiments of Martindale's brigade to guard our flank from an approach from Richmond, and to destroy the railroad and telegraph lines running to that city. This command discovered the presence of a large force of rebels at the railroad station, and Martindale's brigade thus became immediately engaged. All this was unknown to the corps commander, who was pressing toward the Court House with the remainder of Morell's division, Butterfield leading. The Twenty-eighth North Carolina, which had retreated toward the Court House, was almost entirely captured by our cavalry under Emory, who at that time, and until he was ordered to return, was accompanied by the Seventeenth New York, under Colonel Lansing.

Thus Martindale was left to meet a sudden attack from Branch's whole command, and it was with difficulty that he could inform General Porter of his exact position, so little was it thought possible for a rebel force to appear on our left and rear. When informed of the critical situation of Martindale's brigade, General Porter ordered the entire command to face about and toward Martindale, left in front.

General Morell, leading his old brigade, now under Colonel McQuade, reached Martindale, who had been forced back to the east of the main road, with the Fourteenth New York in advance, and in time to change the whole face of affairs. This regiment relieved the Second Maine and Forty-fourth New York, who had been nearly overwhelmed by Branch's large brigade, and who were also almost out of ammunition. The remainder of McQuade's brigade moved toward the west *en eschelon* and through the woods, striking Branch on his left and rear; and in conjunction with Martindale, who now pushed forward, completely routed the enemy.

In the meantime Butterfield, brought by Porter's movement into the rear of the column, directed his troops toward the sound of the firing, in two columns—one along the railroad and one by the turnpike. This force came upon the field as the enemy were being driven, but in time to take some prisoners on their left. Griffin's Battery "D" Fifth United States Artillery, Martin's Battery "C" Massachusetts Artillery, and Benson's battery were warmly engaged for some hours. On the rebel side the troops were mainly of Branch's North Carolinians, but General Porter reports that Georgia troops were present. These latter must have belonged to R. H. Anderson's brigade, which had fallen back from the front of General McDowell then advancing from Fredericksburg. Branch's command must have been about 10,000 strong.

The objects of the expedition were accomplished, and the destruction of bridges and railroads as far as Ashland being completed, General Porter returned to his old camps.

CHAPTER VI.

BATTLE OF FAIR OAKS.

MEANWHILE McClellan was moving steadily toward the rebel capital. On May 20th Naglee's brigade, of Casey's division, crossed the Chickahominy at Bottom's Bridge, and, three days later, the remainder of the corps, the Fourth, followed under General Keyes. On the 25th it took up a position at the Seven Pines, on the main turnpike leading to Richmond, about five miles from the city. The Third Corps, Heintzelman's, also crossed on this date. Hooker's division moved southward to guard the White Oak Swamp Bridge, and Kearny's division took position in advance of Savage's Station. On the left bank of the Chickahominy were Sumner's, Franklin's, and Porter's corps, with General McClellan's Headquarters at Gaines' Mill. The consolidated returns of the army show an aggregate of 126,089 officers and men present on May 31st, with 280 pieces of field artillery.

Serious work was now at hand, and we pass to the incidents of the first bloody and important contest of the campaign, known as the Battle of Fair Oaks or Seven Pines.

Johnston, who was in communication with Jackson, and probably felt certain that the junction of McDowell would be attempted as the best way to utilize that force, and as suggested by military prudence, resolved to anticipate the event and strike McClellan before he was reinforced by so formidable a body of fresh troops. He had made all necessary dispositions for an attack. Huger's division of three brigades was moved up from Petersburg. A. P. Hill's was ordered to march to the north of the Chickahominy at Meadows Bridge and to remain on that side of the stream. General Smith was directed to place his division on the left of Magruder's on the Mechanicsville turnpike, that he, the second officer in rank, might be in position to command on the left. Longstreet's division was placed on the left of that of D. H. Hill, and Huger's in rear of the interval between those last named. It was intended that Smith and A. P. Hill should move against the Union right, that Magruder and Huger, crossing by New Bridge, should form between the left wing and the Chickahominy, while Longstreet's and D. H. Hill's, their left thrown forward, assailed the right flank of the two corps on the Williamsburg road and on the Richmond side of the stream. Johnston supposed that the bridges and fords would furnish sufficient means of communication between the two parts of the Confederate army. Such are the words used by General Johnston in his narrative. It is true that he writes after the fact, but it is plain that he had no fear as to the result of an encounter with the whole of McClellan's force, and also that he did not regard the Chickahominy as a barrier to prompt and easy communication between the two wings of his own army, which, by this plan of battle, would be divided by that stream. While the generals of division were with Johnston to receive his final instructions for this attack, the expediency of which was urged before the accession of McDowell's large and fresh corps, General Stuart, who had a small force of cavalry watching McDowell at Fredericksburg, reported that the force, which had been marching southward, had turned back, indicating a change of intention by the two portions of the Federal army. This intelligence caused

General Johnston to begin the offensive at once and attack the two Federal corps on the south of the Chickahominy at Fair Oaks as soon as they had advanced far enough to put a sufficient interval between themselves and the three corps on the left bank of the river. On the morning of the 30th, by orders of General D. H. Hill, a reconnoissance in force was made by Brigadier-General Rodes on the Charles City road, and by Brigadier-General Garland on the Williamsburg road. General Rodes met no enemy, but General Garland encountered Federal outposts more than two miles to the west of Seven Pines, in numbers sufficient to indicate the presence of a corps at least. Of this Johnston was informed about noon and at once told General Hill to prepare for an attack the next morning. Orders were promptly given to concentrate twenty-three out of twenty-seven brigades of the rebel army against the two Union corps, about two-fifths of McClellan's army. The four others were observing the river from New Bridge up to Meadow Bridge. Longstreet and Huger were directed to move to D. H. Hill's position as early as possible next morning, and Smith to march with his brigade to the point of meeting of the New Bridge and Nine Mile roads, near which Magruder had five brigades.

Longstreet, the ranking officer of the three divisions to be united near Hill's camp, was instructed verbally to form his own and Hill's division in two lines of attack at right angles to the Williamsburg road, and Huger was instructed to advance down the Charles City road until he reached a point opposite, and in the rear of the Federal left flank, to attack as soon as he became aware that they were fully engaged in front. In case abatis or entrenchments were encountered, the troops were ordered to turn them. General Smith was to engage reinforcements should any be sent across the Chickahominy; and, in case he should encounter none, to attack on the left of the troops already engaged. Although the second in command, General Smith was not transferred to the point of first attack, lest the delay in moving his troops from the left, where they lay, should take up valuable time.*

Let us turn to the Federal side, and study the disposition of the left wing, advanced and cut off from support, as Johnston supposed it was, after the passage of the Chickahominy. On the 24th General Naglee led a reconnoissance in force from the camp near Bottom's Bridge, and penetrated as far along the right bank of the river as the woods next beyond Savage's Station, where he met a strong body of the rebels, consisting of infantry, cavalry, and artillery, under command of General Stuart. As he reports, a conflict ensued, which resulted in the enforced abandonment of their position by the rebels.

On the 27th the troops again moved forward, and supported the advanced picket-line, which was within about five miles of Richmond. The Eleventh Maine and One Hundred and Fourth Pennsylvania held this honorable and exposed position, which they maintained until the 31st, when they met the first force of the enemy's attack. General Keyes, commanding the corps, was ordered to select and fortify a strong position on the Richmond road. He accordingly commenced a line near Savage's Station, a mile and a half behind Seven Pines. This is the work mentioned by General Couch, in his diary, on the 27th, where he speaks of a strong entrenched line constructed by his men, under orders of General McClellan—the position of which is shown on the map. As it was deemed important by the commanding general that the position of Seven Pines—the junction of the Williamsburg road with the Nine Mile road—should be strongly held, Lieutenant McAllester was directed by General Barnard, Chief of Engineers, to fortify the ground.

* But he went to that point and remained there.

He selected a position a mile and a half in advance of the Seven Pines, which he deemed tenable, and which was visited by General Barnard on the 28th, who directed the commencement of a redoubt, rifle-pits, felling of trees, etc. McAllester was unable to procure men enough to throw up rapidly an adequate defensive line, and the redoubt was un-

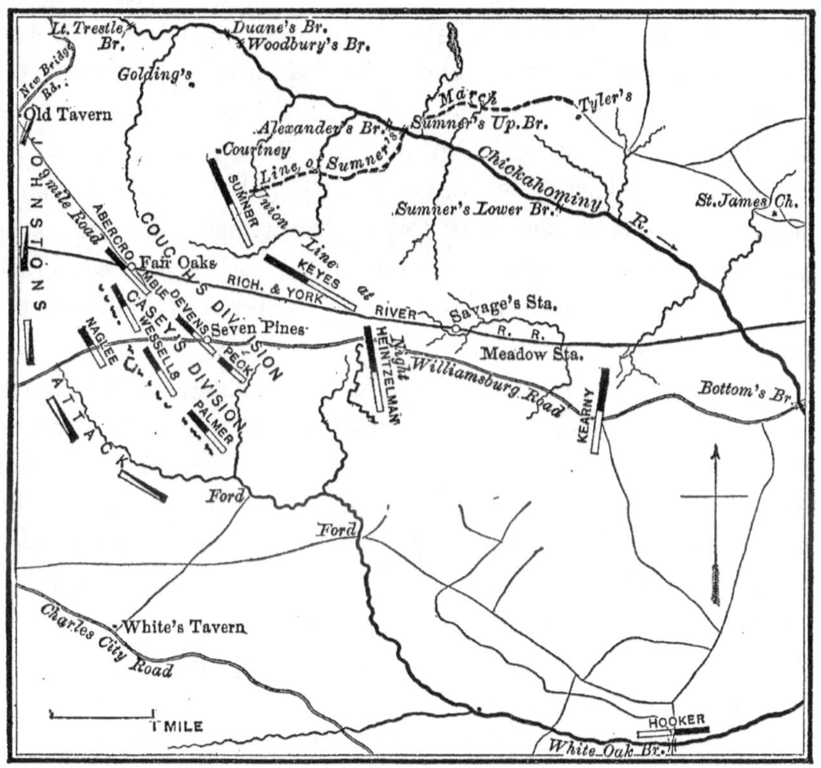

Battle-field of "Fair Oaks."

finished at the time of the attack. The brigades composing Casey's Second Division, Fourth Corps, which occupied the advance of this wing, covered only by the unfinished works above described, were, respectively: 1st, Naglee on the right; 2d, Wessels in the centre; 3d, Palmer on the left. The First Division, Couchs', consisted of: 1st, Peck's Brigade; 2d, Abercrombie's; 3d, Devens'. The corps numbered on the muster-rolls about 12,000 men, of all arms, but no more than two-thirds were present fit for duty on May 31, 1862.

General Keyes expected, and was preparing for, a battle. Couch in his diary notes that he was sending back wagons to the north side of the river. His own division was encamped at Seven Pines about half a mile in the rear of Casey's, of whom he speaks, saying that Casey's pickets were skirmishing hotly on the 29th, and that the enemy were threatening both flanks of the corps. On the 30th he notes that the skirmishing was so severe in Casey's front that at his request a part of Peck's brigade was sent to him. This is the reconnoissance mentioned by Johnston, which determined the time and manner of his attack.

It will readily be seen that there was nothing in the nature of a surprise about the rebel attack on the 31st. The commanding officers were on the alert, and everything indicated that a few hours at the latest would open the contest. But before the strife of men began the elements joined battle. On the night of the 30th and 31st there was a storm of tropical violence, which is mentioned in all the reports. It is not often that, within the limits of the stern brevity required by a military report, any allusion is made such as the fury of this storm drew from General Keyes, who in speaking of it, says: "From their beds of mud and the peltings of this storm the Fourth Corps rose to fight the battle of May 31, 1862." At about ten o'clock in the morning, Lieutenant Washington, an aide-de-camp of General Johnston's, was captured by the Federal pickets in an open field to the right of Fair Oaks, which was the extremity of General Casey's line, and brought before General Keyes. As the enemy appeared to be in force on the right, Keyes anticipated the weight of attack from that quarter. He gave orders to have the troops under arms at eleven o'clock and rode over to Fair Oaks Station, meeting on the way Colonel Bailey, chief of artillery, whom he ordered to put his guns in readiness for action. Finding nothing unusual at Fair Oaks he returned toward Seven Pines, and as the firing in front of Casey grew more brisk, as a precaution, he ordered Couch to send Peck's Brigade to his support.

At about 12.30 P.M. it became suddenly manifest that the attack was made in great force and General Keyes sent at once to General Heintzelman for reinforcements. His message was delayed and it was not until 3 P.M. that Berry's and Jamieson's brigades of Kearny's division reached the scene of action.* Casey's division was in front of the abatis and his pickets about one thousand yards beyond, it being impossible to extend them farther because the ground immediately in front of that point was held by the enemy in force. The pickets, reinforced by the One Hundred and Third Pennsylvania, soon broke and, joined by a large number of sick, camp followers and skulkers, flowed in a steady stream to the rear, thus giving the impression that Casey's division had broken in a panic, and left the field without making any firm or prolonged resistance. So strong was that impression, that General McClellan, who did not make his appearance on the ground until the next day, telegraphed to Mr. Stanton: " Casey's division, which was the first line, gave way unaccountably and discreditably." In his report, made at a later day, he retracted this injurious expression, but for some time this division, which, as will be shown, fought well and lost heavily, remained under the gravest accusations of cowardice. An examination in detail of the reports of the brigade commanders, will show the facts. Palmer reports

*Kearny led with Berry's Brigade.

that the Third Brigade, composed of new troops, was in a poor state of discipline, not controlled by the officers. About 400 were detailed on picket duty, and were stragglers; the remainder, about 1,000 strong, were attacked in front and on both flanks, and after returning the enemy's fire with spirit, fell back to the woods in their rear. The Eighty-first New York lost its colonel, major, one captain, and many men killed. Colonel Hunt of the Ninety-second was wounded and obliged to leave the field. The regiments were scattered; the smoke made it impossible to observe more than one regiment at a time, and when Palmer applied for reinforcements he was told to fall back on the new line formed in the rear. He claims his loss to have been about one-fourth of the number engaged, and blames those who placed a small force of the rawest men in the army in the most exposed position to bear the brunt of an attack.

General Wessels reports that of an actual effective force in his brigade of 1,500 men, 34 were killed, 271 wounded, and 55 missing, and tells the same story of stubborn resistance, that regiment after regiment, enveloped by superior numbers and enfiladed on both flanks, fell back from position to position, until at nightfall, having been driven from the last post to which he had been assigned on the right of Devens, he encamped near Savage's Station.

General Naglee was more fortunate in two respects, the quality of his men and the result of the action; for although he with the others was compelled to fall back, it would seem that they made a more stubborn resistance, favored in some respects by the nature of the ground, and by the fact that they were enabled to form a junction with the reinforcements brought up on the right. At about one o'clock, by order of General Casey, the One Hundredth New York, One Hundred and Fourth Pennsylvania, and Eleventh Maine, made a charge on the enemy in their front. Passing over a rail fence they came into the open held by the rebels, where the fire became hotter than before, Spratt's battery taking an active part. By this time the left of Casey's command had been forced back upon the position of Couch, the colonel of the One Hundredth New York was killed, that of the One Hundred and Fourth was wounded, half the men were killed and wounded, and the enemy, constantly reinforced, pressed them so closely that Sergeant Porter, left guide of the One Hundred and Fourth, was struck over the neck with a musket. Orders were given to retire. The horses of one of Spratt's guns being killed, the piece was abandoned. All this time the men had been fighting in front of the intrenchment. Now, as they fell back, an opportunity was afforded to Colonel Bailey, of the First New York artillery, who promptly ordered the batteries of Fitch and Bates to open on the rebels as they pressed forward in pursuit. The order was obeyed with so good effect of grape and canister, that although repeatedly urged to the assault and coming up with courage, such was their loss that the enemy fell back from this point.

A little later the rebels advanced on the left and in the rear of the redoubt, and stationed sharpshooters in the trees in such position as to command that point and the rifle-pits. Here their fire at short range was most fatal and effective. Colonel Bailey was shot through the head while directing the batteries in the redoubt and giving instructions as to spiking the guns if abandoned. Major Van Valkenberg, of the same regiment, was killed shortly after, Adjutant Rumsey wounded, and the batteries left without officers, and in the course of the next hour it was necessary to leave the guns, most of the horses having been killed, with the exception of a part of Regan's battery, which was brought off, the men supporting the wounded horses to keep them from falling in the traces. The rebels now turned the guns left in the redoubt upon the left flank of the Fifty-sixth New York, Eleventh Maine, and Fifty-second Pennsylvania. This with the fire in front was not to be endured, and they were withdrawn and put in position in the rear of the Nine Mile road, about three hundred yards from the Seven Pines. This line was held till toward dark, when the enemy, advancing in masses down the rear of the Nine Mile road, compelled a general retrograde movement, which did not stop till all arrived at a new line of defence, one mile in the rear.

The report of General Keyes shows that he was called upon early in the action to reinforce the first line, and did so until he had so far depleted the second that he could not with safety weaken it farther. He bears testimony to the determined gallantry with which the majority of Casey's division held its ground, only giving way when overwhelmed by masses of the enemy. Under his direction, with the assistance of Generals Naglee and Devens, a change of front of the troops on the Williamsburg road was effected, by which a line in the rear of the Nine Mile road was formed, which proved so firm a barrier to the advance of the rebels, and which finally fell back in good order to the line near Savage's Station.

About 4.12 P.M., seeing the enemy advancing in overwhelming numbers on the right, General Keyes himself hastened to the left to bring up reinforcements, and with the assent of General Heintzelman sent forward General Peck with the One Hundred and Second, and Ninety-third Pennsylvania regiments. Colonels Rowley and McCarter were ordered to advance across the open space to attack. They advanced under a heavy fire, and formed in a line oblique to the Nine Mile road, where they maintained their position for half an hour, doing great execution. Compelled at length to give way, Peck and the One Hundred and Second crossed the Williamsburg road to the wood, and McCarter, with the bulk of the Ninety-second, passed to the right, where they took part in the last line of battle, formed about 6 P.M. Colonel Briggs, of the Tenth Massachusetts, under orders from General Keyes, led his regiment in face of a heavy fire and formed with the precision of parade on the right of this last mentioned line. It was a most favorable position, being in a wood without much undergrowth, where the ground sloped somewhat abruptly to the rear. Had the regiment been two minutes later, this fine position would have been lost, and it would have been impossible to form the last line which stemmed the tide of defeat and made victory possible. This success was begun here by the Fourth Corps and the two brigades of Kearny's division. When this position was taken, it was observed that the left of the line was dwindling away, * that the artillery had withdrawn, that the centre was weakening, and large bodies of rebels were pouring down the Williamsburg road to the rear. Generals Keyes, Heintzelman, and others passed through the opening of the entrenchments of the 28th, and by strenuous efforts rallied a number of men, and induced them to turn about and join a line better organized, posted in the woods, and formed perpendicular to the road, and advanced some sixty yards to the left of the road toward the field where the battle had been confined for more than two hours against vastly superior numbers. The line was formed of companies, regiments, and parts of regiments, fragments of divisions and brigades which had lost their integrity in the fierce fight of the afternoon. Casey, Couch, Kearny, Birney were all represented, and the men stood firm, shoulder to shoulder, in the fading light.

*Berry's Brigade and the Sixty-third and One Hundred and Fifth Pennsylvania, regiments of Johnson's Brigade were cut off and fought until dark, losing heavily, but holding in check the rebel right.

In the course of the two hours preceding these events, three Pennsylvania batteries under Major West (Flood's, McCarty's and Miller's) of Couch's division, did admirable service. Miller's in particular, from its central position, threw shell with great precision over the heads of our troops, which fell into the masses of the enemy, and later, when the enemy were rushing in upon the right, he threw case and canister among them, doing frightful execution. This substantially closes the action of May 31st, as to that portion of it which was fought in front of Casey's division, and in which the troops of Keyes' and Heintzelman's corps participated. Of these, every division except the Second Division of Hooker was heavily engaged during the long hours from 12.30 to 6.30 P.M. Early in the afternoon, when the first weight of the rebel assault was thrown upon Casey's right, which had been driven back upon Couch's division, the latter, by the weight and impetus of the charge, was cut off from his command with Abercrombie and four regiments with a battery and prisoners. After endeavoring to cut his way back to his main force and finding the odds against him too great, he withdrew toward the Grape Vine Bridge on the Chickahominy, and took a position facing Fair Oaks.

So McClellan's promising advance toward Richmond received an unexpected repulse. Keyes' Corps and half of Heintzelman's, which had reinforced him, had been driven back a mile.

Let us return for a moment to the rebel side and see what were the reasons for the partial failure of their admirably formed plan of attack upon two comparatively weak corps of McClellan's army, separated from their comrades by the treacherous Chickahominy. Their order of battle, it will be remembered, put G. W. Smith on the left, Johnston being with him, Longstreet and D. H. Hill in the centre, and Huger on the right, with orders to move on the left flank and rear of the Federals. Some recrimination was indulged in by the commanding officers, on account of the delay on Longstreet's part in making the attack, and the alleged total failure of Huger to co-operate at all.

While the long time which elapsed, after the attack was begun by Hill and before Smith co-operated, formed the subject of criticism, it is urged on behalf of Huger that his troops were unaccustomed to marching, having been in garrison duty so long at Norfolk, and that finding the road heavy and the swamp overflowed, they were unable to take position in time to be of any service. Huger for himself says that his instructions were not positive, and that he was not informed of the place of attack. General Johnston has charged as follows: "Had General Huger's division been in position and ready for action when those of Smith, Longstreet, and Hill moved, I am satisfied that Keyes' corps would have been destroyed instead of merely defeated. Had it gone into action at even four o'clock the victory would have been much more complete." Huger replied in his demand for a court of inquiry: "To the last paragraph I have only to say that if it did not go into action by four o'clock, it was because General Longstreet did not require it, as it was in position and awaiting his orders. Four of the brigades had been sent for and did go into action on Saturday afternoon—three of Longstreet's and one of Huger's—the other two were in position and could have gone if ordered." Johnston's report ignores the presence of Huger's division at any part of the action. This request for a Court of Inquiry by Huger, addressed to Jefferson Davis, as President, through George W. Randolph, Secretary of War, was referred to General Johnston and indorsed by Davis favorably, unless General Longstreet's reply "will enable Johnston to relieve Huger of his grievance." Huger seems to have defended himself successfully.

As to Smith, on the other hand, a cause for the delay in his attack is found in a peculiar condition of the elements. Although General Johnston was only separated from General Longstreet at the centre by a brief interval of three miles or more, he left the time of the commencement of the action by the latter to be determined by the sound of the musketry which he supposed would be distinctly audible at his position, instead of making certain of the fact by means of an aide who could have brought him the news of Hill's advance the moment the order was given. The wind proved an unreliable courier; it took up the sound of the cannon and carried that only to Johnston and Smith. It was not until Hill's movement had resulted in a heavy engagement which had lasted for some hours that, about three o'clock P.M., Smith was informed of the state of affairs and pushed in on Couch's right, cutting the latter off from the remainder of his division. These mistakes on the part of the enemy saved us from a more serious disaster than we suffered.

Upon the Union side there are other and more satisfactory incidents of the day to be noticed.

General McClellan's headquarters at this time were at Gaines' Mill, on the opposite side of the Chickahominy. Hearing the firing at Keyes' front, he ordered Sumner, then encamped with his corps near Tyler's house, on the same side of the stream, to be in readiness to march at a moment's warning. Sumner instantly put his men under arms, and, at two o'clock, General Sedgwick's division left camp and advanced to the upper bridge, where they halted to await further orders. At half-past two orders to march to the support of Heintzelman were received, and the column was at once pushed forward, Gorman's brigade in advance, followed by Kirby's battery; then Burns' and Dana's brigades, followed by Tompkins', Bartlett's, and Devens' batteries. The river had risen during the night and morning, the causeways approaching the bridge on either side were overflowed, and the bridges, trembling under the strong current which covered the planking, were in momentary danger of destruction; and it was not till the weight of the marching column steadied Sumner's upper bridge that confidence was felt that the structure would stand. The utmost difficulty was experienced in getting the guns along; it was necessary to unlimber and use the prolongs, the men tugging at the mired pieces up to their waists in water. Of Richardson's division, French's brigade only was able to cross at the lower bridge, and Howard's and Meagher's brigades were obliged to cross by the upper bridge, opposite General Sedgwick's camp. Sedgwick's advance—the First Minnesota, Colonel Sully, leading—arrived on the field about 4.30 P.M., and found Abercrombie's command, of Couch's division, southwest of Courtney's house,* hard pressed by the enemy. Colonel Sully formed his regiment on his right. Gorman's brigade formed on Abercrombie's left, becoming hotly engaged; it was charged by the enemy, who were repulsed; when charging in turn, it drove them from their position. Kirby's battery arrived on the field, and, with three pieces and one caisson, was put into action on the left. Soon Lieutenants French and Woodruff arrived with three more pieces; the caisson was in the rear, buried in the mud; the trail of one gun broke at the fourth discharge. The enemy prepared to charge on Kirby's right, but he changed front to the right, and sent back two limbers to the caisson for ammunition, firing round shot in the meantime. The enemy came down a road, and found themselves in front instead of to right of Kirby's guns, and exposed to a fire of canister from five

* To which position it had been removed by General Couch from Fair Oaks; and upon it the Second Corps formed. It was never driven by the rebels.

light 12-pounders, and were compelled to retreat to the woods in disorder; the recoil buried the guns to their axles in the mud; at one time three pieces were in that condition, and were only extricated with the aid of the Fifteenth Massachusetts Volunteers. This battery was the only one which arrived in time to take part in the action at this point. Generals Burns and Dana were prompt to arrive, the latter with only two regiments, the Twentieth Massachusetts and Seventh Michigan, the other two, the Nineteenth Massachusetts and Forty-second New York, having been left behind, the one on picket, the other to protect the crossing and assist the passage of the artillery. General Dana soon after went into action on the left of Gorman's brigade, and took part in a brilliant charge. General Burns took post on the right of Colonel Sully with two regiments, holding two in reserve—the Seventy-second Pennsylvania, Colonel Baxter, overlapping Colonel Sully's right, and the Sixty-ninth Pennsylvania, Colonel Owens, on his right and rear, covering the right of the road from Courtney's to Golding's house. During the night the Seventy-first Pennsylvania, and First California of this division, with the Nineteenth Massachusetts, Sixty-third and Forty-second New York were ordered back toward the Chickahominy, to hold the line of communication and protect the ammunition and artillery, nearly all of which was mired on the south side of the river.

The troops to whom this line was opposed during the latter part of the day were Hood's brigade, Whiting's, Pettigrew's, Hampton's, and Hatton's, and the attacks upon Kirby's battery were made successively by Whiting, Pettigrew, and Hampton. General Hampton reports that after driving the enemy a short distance through the woods, he found that they were being rapidly reinforced and held a strong position either fortified or affording natural shelter, and even fast extending beyond his (Hampton's) left. Upon being informed of the state of affairs by Colonel Lee (rebel) of the artillery, General G. W. Smith, in his report says, that he immediately ordered up Hatton's brigade and Colonel Lightfoot's regiment of Pettigrew's, until then held in reserve, into action upon Hampton's left, where the whole line came within fifteen or twenty yards of the line of the enemy's (Federal) fire, which apparently came from the low bank of an old ditch, either a drain or the foundation of a fence very near the surface of the ground. Various attempts were made to charge the enemy, but for want of concert all failed. In this engagement the rebel loss as reported by General Smith, was 1,283, killed, wounded, and missing. General Pettigrew was wounded and taken prisoner, General Hampton wounded, and General Hatton killed. General Smith expresses the rather sanguine opinion that if he could have had an hour more of daylight, with the assistance of Hood's brigade of Texans on the right, supported by Griffith's of Mississippi on the left, as well as by the brigade of General Simms, all fresh troops, the enemy would have been driven into the swamps of the Chickahominy. As it was, darkness compelled him to relinquish "an unfinished task," a task, it may be here said, which was still unfinished the next day, when he had all the advantages to be derived from daylight and opportunity.

Three times in his report of this day's action General Smith speaks of the enemy's (Federal) strong position, as "either fortified or offering natural shelter"; again the "strong position of the enemy is better understood"; again, "reconnoisance made during the morning developed the fact that the enemy (Federal) were strongly fortified in the position attacked by my division on the previous evening."

There was no fortification, or the semblance of one, on any part of the line held by the fragment of Couch's division under General Abercrombie* and the troops of Sumner's corps as they arrived on the field in the afternoon; the only artillery on the ground was a section of Brady's battery and Kirby's First Artillery, which was posted in the open field near Adams' house; the remainder of the artillery of Sumner's corps came on the ground only in time to be used in the action of the next morning. The imaginary fortified position which Smith encountered was, in fact, the living wall of brave men who withstood his advance and compelled him finally to retreat. The First Division of Sumner's Corps, General Richardson's, did not arrive on the field until the firing in Couch's and Sedgwick's division had ceased, it being then dark.

On reporting to Sumner, Richardson was ordered to take position on the line of the railroad, on the left of General Sedgwick, and to communicate with the pickets of General Birney on the left. The brigade of General French was placed on the railroad, three regiments of General Howard in second line, three regiments of General Meagher in third line, and one of General Howard's, the Fifth New Hampshire, as the advance guard to General French. The men bivouacked under arms, and one regiment of General Meagher's command, the Sixty-third New York, was sent back, with General Sumner's permission, to try and get up at least two pieces of artillery before morning. The Fifth New Hampshire during the night were within half musket shot of the Second and Fifth Texas; the Second Mississippi, upon whom General Smith relied to take the enemy's (Federal) fortifications the next morning, were withdrawn before daylight. At two o'clock of the morning of June 1st, a council of war was held in General Sumner's tent, and it was re-

* Thirty-first Pennsylvania, Sixty-fifth New York, Sixty-first Pennsylvania, Sixty-second New York, Seventh Massachusetts—portions of three brigades.

solved to attack the enemy as soon as disposition for that purpose could be made.

Again glancing at the entire operations of the day, we find the situation relieved by the conduct of Sumner,* who came on the field in time to restore our line on the right, and check the further progress of the enemy. The exertions of Keyes, Heintzelman, and their officers and men were thus prevented from proving futile. The rebels pouring down in great numbers to drive us into the Chickahominy had failed of their object.

On the following morning, June 1st, the battle was renewed, and ended with success of the Union troops and the re-establishment of the lines lost the previous day.

About sunset on May 31st, General J. E. Johnston, Commander-in-Chief of the rebel army, who had been shortly before wounded by a bullet in the shoulder, was struck from his horse by a shell, and severely injured and carried from the field. The command devolved upon General G. W. Smith, second in rank, who directed operations until June 2d, when General R. E. Lee was placed in command of the Army of Northern Virginia, a position which he held with honor until April, 1865. On the morning of June 1st, the rebels took the initiative, and about 5 o'clock A.M. a column of cavalry and a line of infantry pickets were seen deploying in an open field on the right of the position held by General Richardson. If this was intended, as he thinks, for the head of a real attack, it was broken up and driven back by Captain Pettit's battery, which had just come on the field, and no further attempt was made from that direction. Finding that a gap existed between General French's left and the right of General Birney, which was unoccupied, and exposed the line to be cut at this point, General Richardson moved General French three battalions' length to the

* Report of Couch, p. 174, War Records.

left, and put in a regiment of General Howard's still farther to the left, and the Fifth New Hampshire in second line. Hardly had these arrangements been completed, when about 6.30 A.M. a furious fire of musketry began from a distance of about fifty yards. Near our left two roads crossed the railroad, and up these the enemy moved his column of attack, supported on his left by battalions deployed in line of battle in the woods, the whole line coming up at once without any skirmishers in advance. Our men returned the fire with vivacity, and the fire soon became the heaviest yet experienced, the enemy putting in fresh regiments five times to allow their men to replenish ammunition. This lasted for an hour and a half, when the enemy, unable any longer to bear the fire, fell back, but in the course of half an hour renewed the contest with reinforcements, when an action of about one hour's duration ensued, at the end of which time the division charged on the enemy in their front, supported at the moment by a charge upon their left and rear, led by General French in person, and compelled them to fall back, their retreat being precipitated by the fire of four guns of Pettit's battery. The division lost about 900 killed, wounded, and missing.

General Sickles, in his report of the advance on June 1st, says the fields were strewn with Enfield rifles marked "Tower, 1862," and muskets marked "Virginia" thrown away by the enemy in his sudden retreat. In the camp occupied by Generals Casey and Couch were found rebel caissons filled with ammunition, a large number of small arms, and several baggage wagons, besides two barns filled with subsistence and forage.

The attempt of the rebels to drive the left wing into the Chickahominy, and cut McClellan's line of supply from White House, which opened with every prospect of success, was turned first into failure and then into disaster, which sent them back to Richmond in a panic on the night of June 1st.

General Johnston, who refers in his report to the entrenchments which prevented General G. W. Smith from attacking the right of Sumner's line on June 1st, claims a victory on that day, when he was not on the field, and on the 31st, he alleges that his forces took 10 guns, 6,000 muskets, 1 garrison flag, and 4 regimental colors, and many hundred prisoners, and states his total loss to have been 4,283.

D. H. Hill, who led the advance on Casey's camp, claims to have driven the Union troops first a mile and a half, and subsequently a mile further, meeting with a constant series of successes on May 31st and June lst, until, by reason of the "Yankees" occupying ground in his rear on the Nine Mile road (a strange place for a beaten enemy to be in), it was deemed best to withdraw to Richmond.

CHAPTER VII.

WITHDRAWAL TO THE JAMES. — THE "SEVEN DAYS' BATTLE."

AFTER the battle of Fair Oaks there was a pause in active operations in front of Richmond, partly owing to the exhaustion consequent upon that event, and partly to the weather, which for the next two weeks was unfavorable to such a degree as to render any advance almost impossible. All the bridges had been carried away; the wings of the Union army were separated by the river, and on the only avenue of supply for the three corps on the right bank, the railroad bridge and trestlework were threatened with momentary destruction; the ground, which consisted of alternate layers of reddish clay and quicksand, had turned into a vast swamp, and the guns in battery sank into the earth by their own weight. That most arduous of tasks in inclement weather, entrenching, occupied the interval. The line laid out beyond Seven Pines by the Engineer Corps was strengthened and completed from Golding's to White Oak Swamp.

Changes were made in the disposition of the troops. The front at Seven Pines was heavily reinforced. Franklin's corps was brought over from the other bank of the Chickahominy and posted on the right of the line; on his left was Sumner, and Heintzelman on his left extending toward the White Oak Swamp, with Keyes' corps in reserve. The as-

James Longstreet

signment of General Casey to the command of the supply depot at the White House occasioned some changes in the latter corps, Peck being given Casey's division, now composed of Naglee's and Wessel's brigades. Porter's corps alone remained on the left bank of the Chickahominy in the vicinity of Gaines' Mill, with McCall's division of Pennsylvania reserves, which had come by water from McDowell's corps, posted farther on at Mechanicsville and Beaver Dam Creek.

The rebel force, under command of R. E. Lee, augmented in numbers by drafts on their resources in every direction, was now composed as follows: Longstreet's division—six brigades: Pickett's, Anderson's, Wilcox's, Kemper's, Pryor's, and Featherston's A. P. Hill's division—six brigades: Anderson's, Gregg's, Field's, Pender's, Branch's, and Archer's. D. H. Hill—five brigades: Rodes', Garland's, Anderson's, Colquitt's, and Ripley's Magruder's command—six brigades: Sumner's, Kershaw's, Griffiths', Cobb's, Toombs', and D. R. Jones'. Huger's division—three brigades: Mahone's, Armistead's, and Wright's. Whiting's division—two brigades: his own and Hood's. Jackson's division—three brigades: Winder's, Cunningham's, and Fulkerson's. Ewell's division—three brigades: Elzey's, Trimble's, and Seymour's. Holmes' command—four brigades: Walker's, Ransom's, Daniels', and Wise's. Lawton's brigade, unattached, under General Jackson's command. Total effective, Lee's army, in seven days' battle before Richmond, by one official estimate, 80,762 men.

McClellan's army in the last week of June stood as follows: Five corps—Porter's on the right of the general line facing Richmond, composed of Morell's and Sykes' divisions, with McCall's temporarily attached. Next across the Chickahominy, we have Franklin with the divisions of Smith and Slocum;

then Sumner with the divisions of Richardson and Sedgwick; then Heintzelman with Kearney's and Hooker's divisions, and lastly Keyes in reserve with Couch's and Peck's divisions. Total effectives, 92,500.

There were now to come seven days of almost continuous fighting—a great struggle for the mastery of the situation around Richmond. McClellan foresaw that the crisis was at hand, and he continued to apply for reinforcements. McCall had arrived, and, in addition, some scattering regiments; but the bulk of McDowell's corps, which he still hoped to have with him, was detained in Northern Virginia.

With Richmond less than five miles distant, the Commander-in-chief now prepared to push still nearer.

On June 25th it was determined by McClellan to move the line in front of Seven Pines forward to a large clearing on the other side of a heavily timbered piece of ground, through the middle of which ran a small stream, whose swampy borders had until that time formed the extreme picket line of the opposing forces in that direction. This was known as the affair of Oak Grove. Heintzelman's corps, part of Sumner's, and Palmer's brigade of Keyes' corps, advanced in good order through the timber, met and repulsed a strong force of the enemy, and occupied the position, throwing out pickets within four miles of Richmond. This advance makes manifest the fact that while General McClellan may, and doubtless did, entertain the plan of moving his base of supplies from White House to the James, he was induced to make this latter move by Stuart's cavalry raid on the 11th rather than with any intention of changing his line of attack or transferring his army to that point.

It is at this point that we reach the crisis of the Peninsula campaign. Despite delays, drawn battles, losses, and unlooked-for natural obstacles, McClellan had succeeded, as he had promised, in reaching the vicinity of the rebel capital—thus relieving Washington, alarming the Southern leaders, and raising the anticipations of the North. It would seem that under this favorable outlook the Government would have strained every nerve to carry the campaign successfully through by reinforcing the army. That its disposition was to do so and reap the advantages of the situation, we believe to be beyond question. It was the fear for the safety of Washington that had caused it to change its strategy at every move of the enemy and produce confusion where system and plan were necessary. It was this fear that retained McDowell at the capital at the opening of the campaign, and it was this fear that withheld him again as he was about to move down from Fredericksburg. And now, once more on June 11th, as Jackson seemed to have ceased his operations in the Shenandoah, McDowell was promised to McClellan, one of whose divisions, under McCall, soon reached the latter.

This promise and expectation of reinforcements in reality proved a hinderance to our success. McClellan called for them, depended upon them, and waited for their arrival. It was so at Yorktown when Franklin joined; it was so again now after Fair Oaks, when McClellan wrote, June 7th, "I shall be in perfect readiness to move forward and take Richmond the moment McCall reaches here and the ground will admit the passage of artillery." That the reinforcements were needed is clear enough; but on the other hand the delay and indecision caused by a dependence upon them gave the enemy the opportunity of forming plans of their own and anticipating those of McClellan. This was obvious now when matters were nearing a crisis: for while McClellan was preparing to strike with his reinforced army (if, indeed, he was not waiting for McDowell and his entire

III.—6

command), Lee and Jackson were devising and executing a scheme which was to put an entirely new face upon the situation.

It is here we encounter the turning-point of the campaign.

Stonewall Jackson was the disturbing factor again. The first suggestion that he might be of use in the immediate operations around Richmond, after the termination of his Valley movements, seems to have come from this officer himself. From Port Republic he wrote to General Johnston as early as June 6th: "Should my command be required at Richmond I can be at Mechanics' Run Depot, on the Central Railroad, the second day's march." Two days later, General Lee noticed the hint and replied to Jackson: "Should there be nothing requiring your attention in the Valley so as to prevent your leaving it for a few days, and you can make' arrangements to deceive the enemy and impress him with the idea of your presence, please let me know, that you may unite at the decisive moment with the army near Richmond." On the 11th he wrote again, and on the 16th a final decision was reached, as appears from the following letter, which, on account of its interest and importance, is here inserted in full:

HEADQUARTERS, NEAR RICHMOND, VA.,
June 16, 1862.

MAJOR-GENERAL T. J. JACKSON,
Commanding Valley District:

General—I have received your letter by the Hon. Mr. Boteler. I hope you will be able to recruit and refresh your troops sufficiently for the movement proposed in my letter of the 11th. You have only acknowledged my letter of the 8th. I am therefore ignorant whether that of the 11th has reached you. From your account of the position of the enemy, I think it would be difficult for you to engage him in time to unite with this army in the battle for Richmond. Fremont and Shields are apparently retrograding, their troops shaken and disorganized, and some time will be required to set them again in the field. If this is so, the sooner you unite with this army the better. McClellan is being strengthened; Burnside is with him, and some of McDowell's troops are also reported to have joined him. There is much sickness in his ranks, but his reinforcements by far exceed his losses. The present, therefore, seems favorable for a junction of your army and this. If you agree with me, the sooner you can make arrangements to do so the better. In moving your troops, you could let it be understood that it was to pursue the enemy in your front. Dispose those to hold the Valley, so as to deceive the enemy, keeping your cavalry well in their front, and at the proper time suddenly descending upon the Pamunkey. To be efficacious, the movement must be secret. Let me know the force you can bring, and be careful to guard from friends and foes your purpose and your intention of personally leaving the Valley. The country is full of spies, and our plans are immediately carried to the enemy. Please inform me what arrangements you can make for subsisting your troops. Beef cattle could at least be driven, and, if necessary, we can subsist on meat alone.

Unless McClellan can be driven out of his intrenchments, he will move by positions, under cover of his heavy guns, within shelling distance of Richmond. I know of no surer way of thwarting him than that proposed. I should like to have the advantage of your views and be able to confer with you. Will meet you at some point on your approach to the Chickahominy. I enclose a copy of my letter of the 11th, lest the original should not have reached you.

I am, with great respect, your obedient servant,

R. E. LEE,
General.

To convey the impression that Jackson was to continue his operations on the Shenandoah, Lee sent him Whiting's and Lawton's brigades from in front of Richmond as reinforcements, and contrived to have the fact reach the Union headquarters. In reality, Jackson took these brigades and Ewell's division of his own command, and, leaving Harrisonburg on the 17th, faced toward Richmond. On the 25th he reached Ashland Station, twelve miles north of the city, having previously met Lee in person and arranged for an immediate, simultaneous, and heavy attack upon McClellan's right wing on the north side of the Chickahominy.

Now upon this same date, the 25th, McClellan and Stanton were telegraphing to each other respecting Jackson's position, the Secretary stating that neither McDowell, Banks, nor Fremont had "any accurate knowledge" in the case, and that among the mass of conflicting rumors his own belief was that Jackson's "real movement" looked toward Richmond. McClellan replied that contrabands coming in on that day reported Jackson's advance at or near Hanover Court House, which confirmed the previously doubted statement of a rebel deserter, that he was certainly moving to take part in a general attack on the Union forces. The doubt remained until the afternoon of the 26th, when McClellan reported that Jackson was driving in his pickets "on the other side of the Chickahominy."

Thus, suddenly, the Army of the Potomac, which was actually pressing toward Richmond, as shown by the affair of Oak Grove on the 25th, found itself thrown again upon the defensive, in the midst of its offensive operations, by Jackson's preconcerted and timely reinforcement of Lee. From this moment we have to follow the fortunes of that army on its *retreat.*

On the other side of the Chickahominy, on the extreme right of the Union line, General McCall had taken position at Mechanicsville on June 19th, with his division, consisting of the brigades of Seymour, Reynolds, and Meade, Cooper's battery of 10-pounder Parrotts, Smead's (regular) four 12-pounders, De Hart's (regular) six 12-pounders, Easton's of four and Kern's of six 12-pounders, both of Pennsylvania. On the 26th, one of his regiments, the Sixth Pennsylvania Reserves, Colonel McKean, was at Tunstall Station, and the Eleventh, Colonel Gallagher, on picket on the lower Chickahominy. On the morning of the 26th, Jackson's advance, Whiting's division, was detained by some Union skirmishers, who destroyed the bridge over Tolopotomoy Creek; but, driving these in, the bridge was repaired, and he pushed on toward McClellan's right and rear.

The position occupied by McCall was naturally strong: its front on the left bank of Beaver Dam Creek, the left on the Chickahominy, the right extending to the thick woods beyond Mechanicsville, which were occupied; on the right of the road crossing at Ellison's Mill, an epaulment for four pieces of field artillery was thrown up, rifle-pits were dug in front of each regiment, and a strong picket-line was maintained from Mechanicsville Bridge to Meadow Bridge. Cooper's and Smead's batteries commanded the right and left approaches of the upper road, and De Hart's battery near the front centre, the same road at a distance, and also the lower road direct to Mechanicsville. The Second Brigade (Meade's) was held in reserve ready to support Reynolds and Seymour, or prevent the enemy from crossing at New Bridge. In view on the opposite side of the Chickahominy were encamped A. P. Hill's division and Cobb's legion of the rebel army, holding strong lines of rifle-pits and two redoubts overlooking the river. About noon on the 26th the enemy was seen to be in motion; at 12.30 the Union pickets at Meadow Bridge were driven in, and line of battle was at once formed. Reynolds, on the right, Seymour on the left, Meade with Easton's and Kern's batteries in reserve.

The rebel General A. P. Hill, whose division, 14,000 strong, was in front of McCall, had, in pursuance of orders, concentrated his division near Meadow Bridge on June 25th. Branch's brigade, with Johnson's battery, was sent to a bridge some seven miles above, where the Brook turnpike crosses the Chickahominy, with orders to communicate with Jackson's advance; and as soon as it had crossed the Central Railroad he was to cross the Chickahominy, take the river road, push on and clear Meadow Bridge, when Hill was at once to cross the bridge, and sweep down to Mechanicsville. Jackson was expected at dawn, but it was ten o'clock before he and Branch communicated, and Branch's advance was delayed by the Union skirmishers. At 3 P.M. General Hill became impatient lest the whole plan should fail, and put his force in motion with six batteries, with four extra horses to each gun. General Field seized the bridge and crossed, meeting but slight opposition; Anderson and Archer followed. Gregg and Pender turned short to the right and moved through the fields to co-operate on the right of the first column. Field's advance was met by a concentric fire of artillery, and forming in line of battle, with Pegram's guns in the centre, forced the Union troops from Mechanicsville, upon their stronghold on the other side of Beaver Dam Creek. McIntosh and Anderson endeavored by a movement to the left to capture a Union battery. Archer, Field, Gregg, and Pender, came into line, but met a terrific artillery fire from the Union line. A direct assault on the position was, as the rebel commanders assert, sure to result in heavy loss, and none was ordered. At this time General Branch came up, and was put in support of those already engaged. An attempt was made to turn our left lower down the creek, which failed disastrously. Two regiments of Ripley's brigade, with Pender's brigade, endeavored to flank the position at Ellison's

Mills, but being exposed to the magnificent Union artillery, were repulsed with heavy loss. In the attempt at the Mills there was prolonged fighting. Hour after hour passed, the enemy constantly putting in fresh men from his superior force. General Morell with Griffin's and Martindale's brigades of his division, and two batteries, came to the support of the right of McCall, and at about sunset Griffin went into action and assisted in compelling the enemy to retire. The latter suffered heavy loss, the Union troops losing not over three hundred men.

The force under General McCall was stationed to observe the bridges over the Chickahominy. The position selected was of great natural and artificial strength, and the turn of the road from Mechanicsville to Meadow Creek Valley, where it runs nearly parallel to it, presented the flank of the enemy to the Union troops, who, upon the advance of the hostile column in heavy force, reserved its fire until the head of the column was nearly across, and then poured it in with such close and destructive effect that the enemy made no further attempt to cross the road. That they held their position so long against superior numbers is proof of the discipline and steady valor of our men. After the firing ceased they lay on their arms, replenishing empty cartridge-boxes, refilling haversacks, and caring for the wounded. The General-in-Chief was with General Porter until one o'clock A.M. Reports from scouts and outposts poured in constantly, all of which corroborated the stories in regard to Jackson's movements, which had been the subject of so much mystery in the army and at Washington. Jackson had been delayed this day and took no part in the action; but his presence was ascertained, and on the next morning McCall was ordered to fall back on Gaines' Mill.

It is to be noticed here that McClellan's base of supplies at the White House had become a source of anxiety, since he seemed to doubt his ability to keep his connection with it secure, and because the rain and mud had rendered the roads almost impassable for wagons. Some time in June, the General called General Porter to a meeting with himself alone, half-way between their respective headquarters, to discuss the advantages of the James River as a base. The conclusion reached was that necessity, and necessity only, would warrant such a movement; that it was dangerous and difficult in the face of such a vigilant foe as General Lee, and a disaster would endanger our cause at home and abroad. The necessity of keeping up a constant threat upon Richmond itself for the purpose of showing our confidence in our strength, was then felt. However, it was considered that the necessity might come, and it was determined that we should be prepared for the emergency.

At this time the enemy had begun to show renewed activity in their field works, portending some movement of importance on their part. For security, General McClellan thereupon determined to send General Averill to the James River with a proper force of topographical engineer officers for the purpose of mapping the country from White Oak Swamp to the James, and for obtaining all information necessary to enable him to make a change of base.

BATTLE OF GAINES' MILL.

The morning of June 27th found the Fifth (Porter's) Corps, composed of Sykes' and Morell's divisions of three brigades each, and Berdan's First United States Sharpshooters armed with breech-loading rifles and supported by several batteries of artillery, with McCall's division withdrawn from Mechanicsville, preparing for battle in the vicinity of Gaines' Mill.

Stories of deserters and natives all agreed that Jackson with an overwhelming force was near by, and that with Longstreet and the two Hills he was about to make an effort to destroy the Army of the Potomac. The past two weeks had been dry and warm; the soil had been changed from clinging mud to dust, which, rising from the advancing columns of the enemy betrayed their line of march for miles. Scouts confirmed the rumors. Porter's force consisted of Morell's division—Griffin's, Martindale's, and Butterfield's brigades; McCall's division—Reynolds', Seymour's, and Meade's; Sykes' division—Buchanan's, Lovell's, and Warren's, in all 17,330 infantry for duty. There were present with him 2,534 artillery, of which, from the very nature of the ground, but a very small portion could be used. Six hundred and seventy-one of the regular cavalry under General Emory were put in position covering the bridges across the Chickahominy and the communications with the rest of the army on the right bank. The line occupied by Porter under orders of the General-in-Chief, lay to the east of Powhite Creek, and was well chosen for defence, but the extent of ground to be held was greater than the disposable force at hand. Further, the men of McCall's and a part of those of Morell's divisions had been engaged with the army for hours on the previous day, and were wearied with the battle and retreat from Mechanicsville. The new line of Porter's troops extended from the extreme right, covering the roads leading from Old and New Cold Harbor to Despatch Station with the McGee house in the rear of the right, the troops here being the division under General Sykes. General Cooke with parts of the First and Fifth Regular Cavalry and Rush's Pennsylvania Lancers watched our left.*

* During the night of the 26th, Sykes' division and Butterfield's brigade of Morell's division retired to what became the battle-field of Gaines' Mill. Butterfield

In front of Morell's right was a small stream flowing southerly toward the Chickahominy—between steep banks—some two hundred yards west of the Watt house, its borders fringed by a growth of heavy timber which disappears as it nears the low land about the river. From the stream the land rises for about three-quarters of a mile to the Adams house, whence it falls off sharply to the river; toward the west it was open and rolling to the Gaines house. On the left front of Morell's position was Boatswain's Swamp. The approaches were covered by dense woods, which furnished cover for the enemy's advance. In anticipation of a retreat many of the wagons had already been sent to the rear and some stores destroyed. The position occupied by Sykes'

---

was posted on the extreme left near the Watt house; Sykes' division on the extreme right, leaving an interval to be filled by the two brigades returning with Morell from Mechanicsville, which they occupied. Martin's Battery "C," Massachusetts Artillery, was posted between Morell and Sykes; a section of Weedon's Rhode Island Battery, under Lieutenant Buckley, occupied an opening through the timber in Martindale's brigade, and a section of Allen's Massachusetts in a like position in General Butterfield's. The rest of the artillery from the nature of the ground could not be brought into action. Kingsbury's regular battery was on the high ground some distance in rear of Morell's left, to command the low ground toward the valley of the Chickahominy. Sykes' batteries were those of Tidball and Weed.

On the morning of the 25th, General Porter ordered General Morell to detail two regiments of not less than 500 men each, to serve under General Stoneman with the cavalry. He detailed the Eighteenth Massachusetts, Colonel Barnes, and Seventeenth New York, Colonel Lansing, who reported to Stoneman immediately, marched with him to the White House—were transported by water to the James River and rejoined Morell at Westover, and thus were not engaged in the six days' battles. Porter thus had less than 18,000 infantry at Gaines' Mill.

General McClellan and some of his staff remained with General Porter at his headquarters, just in rear of the troops engaged at Beaver Dam, until after midnight of the 26th; all the plans for the 27th were then and there arranged, and the position to be held behind Boatswain Swamp Run was then selected, but McClellan did not give the positive order until after he had returned to his own headquarters, where he hoped to hear something further of Jackson's force. The General was also at this time considering the proposition made by General Porter to hold his own at the Beaver Dam line, slightly reinforced, while General McClellan moved the main body of the army upon Richmond. Thus the final order did not reach Porter until three or four o'clock in the morning.

division was known to the enemy as Turkey Hill, the crest of which is some sixty feet higher than the plain, over which the troops of Jackson were obliged to advance for about a quarter of a mile in face of a fire of sharpshooters.

Battle-field of Gaines' Mill.

The infantry line was formed on the slope of the hill, behind a line of light barricades, formed in some parts of felled trees, and in others of rails, knapsacks, and such material as lay at hand.

About two o'clock the enemy's pressure was felt. Jackson's march was more circuitous than that of Hill and Longstreet. The latter had crossed the Chickahominy the previous night, after the battle at Mechanicsville. A. P. Hill, who was in the advance, came upon the Union line near Gaines' Mills. Gregg's division in advance, came up with the Union line and was eager to attack at once, but was wisely restrained. Branch came next and was put in on the right of Gregg; Anderson, Field, and Archer in the order named on Branch's right, with Crenshaw's and Johnson's guns in battery on the left of the road in Gregg's rear.

At half past two o'clock P.M., having communicated with General Longstreet, A. P. Hill sent in his division to the attack, and was soon of the opinion that he had the whole Army of the Potomac in his front; at least he formed that opinion, and expressed it in his report, from the incessant roar of musketry and the continued artillery fire which his attack provoked. The men who held that line were Sykes' and Morell's divisions. For two long hours the struggle lasted and then at length aid came from Longstreet and Jackson. The latter, who had been detained on his march by broken bridges and skirmishers, now came on the ground and at once put his entire force into action. Longstreet, who with his division drawn up in lines, massed behind a crest of a hill, had been held in reserve, was now ordered to Hill's support. Pickett's brigade developed the Union position, and Longstreet with a soldier's instinct saw that a mere feint would not relieve A. P. Hill, and gave orders for a general advance, Anderson's and Pickett's brigades joining in the direct assault with the exception of a portion guarding the right flank of the brigades under Wilcox. Whiting's division coming on the field at this moment, made the rebel line complete, and it was hurled with fury against

Porter's small but compact and determined line. In the general charge now made a Union battery which enfiladed the line of D. H. Hill's advance was taken and held for a short time, when it was recovered. General Ewell pushed forward on the road from Gaines' Mill to McGee's house, but found so stubborn a resistance that after four hours of effort he relinquished the task of proceeding farther, and withdrew about dusk. Some of Winder's brigade essayed a like advance, but, not successful in so great measure as they desired, were prevented by night from proceeding more than a few yards beyond McGee's house.

Later in the afternoon, Slocum's division of Franklin's corps crossed the river, and came to the rescue of Porter's hard pressed men, and for a time the tide of battle was more decidedly in the Union favor. So far no impression had been made on the stubborn line. Hard pushed as our men had been since noon, there had not been a sign of wavering at any point. If victory were not in their grasp, it seemed at least that night would put an end to the conflict, and leave them in possession of the hill. They answered the yell of the advancing rebels as they swarmed out of the woods and across the ravine and over the open, with defiant cheers. On they came, Whiting's division hot and eager; Hood's and McLaws' Texan brigades rushed on, pushing their way through hordes of their own disordered and retreating regiments, which had faltered at the line of fire, which had so far marked the limit of their progress. Would they pass it, or recoil as had all the others who had penetrated so far? As Whiting's brigade made its last rush up the slope, at about 7 P.M., the enemy came on in deployed lines and columns by battalions closed in mass, one battalion immediately behind the other. Each line fired as they came down the hill, as soon as it was unmasked by the line in front. They struck us in that manner.

The line was broken after sundown in or near the centre of Morell's division (where was Martindale's brigade, together with one or two brigades of the Pennsylvania Reserves, and some New Jersey regiments of Slocum's division), and at the very point General Porter considered strongest. Two regiments, presumably taken in the rear, were captured. The regulars and zouaves did not break, but brought up the rear in excellent order, quietly moving off the field. They had resisted Jackson's onslaught. A desperate charge was made by five companies of the Fifth U. S. Cavalry, which only served to add to the confusion. The beaten Union troops fell back slowly and in good order. Jackson reports that there was apprehension of a rally, and Whiting sent back to Longstreet for reinforcements. French and Meagher, of Richardson's division, arrived on the field near dark. Their steady front restored the broken Union line, which fell back under the fire of its own guns, supported by the heavy battery south of the river, to the bridges, which they crossed that night.

Two regiments—one the Second New Jersey, of Slocum's, and the Eleventh Pennsylvania, of McCall's, were captured; having continued on the field after their comrades on either flank had retired, they found themselves surrounded, and were obliged to surrender. The loss in guns was heavy; the horses, in many instances, having been killed, and the infantry supports having broken, many were necessarily abandoned to the enemy; others were captured by Whiting's charge, the gunners standing to their pieces to the last, and falling among them. The total loss in artillery was 22 pieces.

The precise number of the attacking force cannot be ascertained. General Magruder says he was on the south bank of the Chickahominy with 25,000 men on the 27th. If the number of Lee's army, as given by Taylor—80, 762—be assumed as correct, Jackson had for the attack 55,000 men, a number more than sufficient to equalize Porter's advantage of position. Jackson claims the capture of 14 pieces of artillery, and admits a loss of 1,000 men in Whiting's successful charge, and gives an estimate of loss—which he admits is based on incomplete returns—at 3,284. The total loss in Porter's corps, as reported by the division commanders, was 6,000 men. While the battle of Gaines' Mill was in progress, the enemy's force—25,000 strong—under Magruder, by a succession of feints, advanced along different portions of the Union line south of the Chickahominy. Furious outbursts of artillery fire, and a resort to every device known which could lead to the belief that an attack in force was imminent, so engaged the Union generals that, when they were appealed to for reinforcements for Porter, General Franklin answered, "I do not think it prudent to send any more troops from here at present." Sumner sent French and Meagher, but, in announcing the fact, adds, "Everything is so uncertain, that I think it would be hazardous to do it."

Magruder was repeating the tactics of Yorktown, and was in momentary apprehension that the small force would be swept away by the advance of McClellan's left, and that the city would fall into his hands. Magruder says: "I received instructions enjoining the utmost vigilance. I passed the night without sleep. Had McClellan massed his whole force in column and advanced it against any point in our line of battle—as was done at Austerlitz, under similar circumstances, by the greatest captain of any age—though the head of his column would have suffered greatly, its momentum would have insured him success, and the occupation of our works about Richmond, and, consequently, of the city, might have been his reward."

General McClellan had fought an army with one corps; yet so stubborn had been the resistance of that corps that Lee and Jackson both believed, and so reported to Richmond, that they had encountered the bulk of McClellan's force. In addition Jackson says (p. 41, Confederate Reports, vol. iv.): "Although swept from their defences by this rapid and almost matchless display of daring and valor, the well-disciplined Federals continued in retreat to fight with stubborn resistance;" and General Whiting (page 47) adds: "The enemy continued to fight in retreat with stubborn resistance, and it soon appeared that we had to do with his best troops."

Lee and Jackson were convinced that McClellan would endeavor to hold his line of supply by the White House, and that if he fell back it would be by way of the Peninsula, as he had advanced, and acting under this belief, General Ewell, preceded by a cavalry force, advanced down the north side of the Chickahominy to Despatch Station and destroyed a portion of the railroad track on the 28th, and on the 29th moved to Bottom's Bridge, when he was recalled to join in the operations above. In the interval the movement on the James, determined on after the battle of Mechanicsville and when the close proximity of Jackson on our right flank was known, had been put into execution. Casey's troops at White House had been ordered down the Pamunkey, via the York and James, to the new base on the latter river. All the material that could not be put on board the transports was burned; the engines and cars, some of the latter loaded with supplies, were put under a full head of steam and were run into the river. The wagons, to the number of five thousand, loaded with everything that could be carried, were set on their way across White Oak Swamp: the reserve artillery took the same road. Twenty-five hundred head of cattle on the hoof were added to this long column. There were few stragglers on that march. What could not be carried away was destroyed. Lines of fire marked the camps and depots of the Union troops. Millions of rations, hundreds of tons of fixed ammunition and shells for the siege guns were thus lost. Lee's uncertainty as to the movements of McClellan, gave the latter twenty-four hours to perfect and carry out his arrangements, and when Lee saw the intentions of the Union General, the retreat was well advanced, and the roads across the swamps guarded to protect the passage of the trains from attack by way of the New Market and Charles City and Williamsburg roads. On the 29th, headquarters were moved from Savage's Station across White Oak Swamp, and on the same day at daylight, Sumner abandoned the works at Fair Oaks and fell back to Orchard Station, where the mass of stores accumulated for the army was destroyed.

BATTLE OF ALLEN'S FARM.

Sumner's and Heintzelman's corps bivouacked on the morning of June 29th at the Allen farm, their forces being disposed fronting Richmond, across the railroad. Richardson, Sedgwick, and Heintzelman from right to left in the order named. General French of Richardson's division held the first line, Caldwell in his rear; a log house in front of Richardson was occupied by Colonel Brooks of the Thirty-seventh Pennsylvania, and immediately in the rear, on a rising piece of ground, four pieces of Hazzard's battery were posted.

Pettit's battery of this division had been sent in advance to Savage's Station with their own and Hazzard's caissons.

These were soon brought back, before Hazzard's limbers were empty, and aided materially in repelling the enemy's attack, which was made with infantry and a battery of artillery, their principal efforts being directed against the position held by Colonel Brooks, who, reinforced by the Seventy-first Pennsylvania of Sedgwick's division, held his own. This attack was made by Griffiths' brigade of Magruder's division, and Jones' division, marching from Golding's across the swamp. Skirmishers were thrown out in front of the rebel divisions, and Jones' men reported the enemy in his front and fortified. Magruder gave orders to remove an obstruction on the railroad so as to permit the passage of a heavy rifled gun, mounted on a railway carriage. Magruder found his reception a warm one, and went in person to bring up reinforcements. But Generals Jackson and Huger had been ordered elsewhere by General Lee. Magruder states that he was suddenly reduced from an expected force of thirty-five thousand to thirteen thousand men, and was thus deprived of the force upon which he had relied to capture "a large portion of the enemy." His command was three times repulsed.

As soon as the attack of Magruder ceased, Sumner fell back on Savage's Station. Lee had at this time divined McClellan's retreat, and was pressing forward in pursuit. His plan was as follows: Longstreet's division was to cross the New Bridge and take position on the extreme right so as to intercept McClellan in his attempt to reach James River, Huger's division to march down the Williamsburg road on Magruder's right flank, and Jackson's division to cross the Chickahominy at Grape Vine Bridge, and operate down that river on its right bank, while Magruder pressed in front. When McClellan's army fell back, it destroyed all the bridges over the Chickahominy, and thus retarded Jackson's advance, and detained him during the 28th and 29th in building the Grape Vine Bridge. Meantime the Union troops were urging their retreat across the White Oak Swamp, a region which had become familiar through reconnoissances made under direction of General Casey.

BATTLE OF SAVAGE'S STATION.

On the 29th Franklin's corps, which had been obliged to abandon its camp at Golding's farm on account of the heavy artillery fire kept up by the enemy from the positions which they had secured after the battle on the 27th, had moved by orders of the General-in-Chief to a position in the vicinity of the railroad at Savage's Station, Slocum's division at the station in reserve, Smith to a point between the river and the station, joining on the right with McCall's division, and on the left with Sumner's corps. Slocum was ordered by General McClellan to cross White Oak Swamp. When General Smith arrived on the ground about seven A.M., neither Sumner nor McCall could be found.

Learning from the report of a staff officer that General Sumner was in front and that there was a break of a mile between his right and Franklin's left; that General Sumner was warmly engaged, and that the enemy was crossing in force by a bridge nearly in his own front, and that both his flanks were unsupported, Franklin directed General Smith to fall back to Savage's Station, and sent word to General Sumner and requested him to fall back to the same place, which Sumner immediately did, having kept back Magruder's advance so that his movement was undisturbed.

Line of battle was formed, Franklin on the right, with Hancock of Smith's division thrown on the right into the woods to hold the railroad; Second Brigade, Brooks, in the woods on the left; Third, Colonel Taylor (General Davidson of this brigade being disabled by sunstroke), in reserve. Smith was supported by Osborn's First New York Artillery, which did good service. Sumner's corps joined on Franklin's left, Richardson on the right, Sedgwick on the left. Heintzelman had withdrawn his corps, 15,000 strong, much to the astonishment of Sumner, who had ordered him to take position on his own left. His reason for so doing is that he saw that the open space about Savage's Station was so crowded with troops that there was no room for more to be usefully employed, and that as there was but one road through the swamp direct from Savage's, he judged it wise to retire by that, after destroying the cars and supplies collected at Savage's Station. The force of the enemy which attacked at this point was that of Magruder, which had been in Sumner's front in the morning, and the same rifled gun on car-wheels figures in this battle. The rebels advanced under cover of the woods, and were several times held in check by the vigorous artillery fire from our side. General Sumner in his report states, "The assault was met by Burns' brigade in the most gallant manner." Hazzard's, Kirby's, Tompkins', Petit's, Osborn's, and Bramhall's batteries were all engaged. A short time before sunset the enemy made an advance along our whole line, coming up with a rush in the face of the heavy fire which was poured into them. The roar of musketry now became steady and continuous, and was maintained for about half an hour, when our troops made several charges and pressed them so hard that their line at length gave way and left the road to the swamp open. Our men, as soon as their officers had restored order and the wounded had been properly cared for, moved out on the retreat. The rebels admit a loss of 4,000, and give that of the Union troops as 3,000.

At this point was situated the great hospital, containing 2,500 sick and wounded, with vast supplies of hospital stores, which was abandoned, and, with the medical men, surgeons, and attendants, who remained behind, to the number of 500, fell into the hands of Jackson, who arrived the next morning, having repaired the bridges across the Chickahominy the previous night, and who now pressed forward in pursuit of the retiring Union men. General Magruder passed by way of the Darbytown road and is next heard of at Malvern Hill.

On the afternoon of the 29th the Commander-in-Chief ordered Keyes' to move during the night to the James River, to occupy a defensive position near Malvern Hill, communicate with the gunboats, and cover Turkey Bridge, Porter to follow and form on his right. Keyes fortunately discovered an abandoned road running parallel with the Quaker road, which he easily opened, and which furnished another way for the trains to pass under cover of the whole line of the army.

The General-in-Chief had passed the day in examining the ground, keeping the trains in motion, and posting troops in such position as to cover their passage from attacks by way of the New Market and Richmond roads. Early in the day there was a sharp skirmish with the rebel cavalry on the Quaker road. This affair is called the skirmish near Willis Church, and showed the danger to which the retreat was exposed, as well as the fact that our line of movement had become known to the enemy. The position of affairs was critical. Longstreet and Hill were almost in contact with Sumner and Franklin by way of the Williamsburg road. Magruder and Huger were coming in on the flank on the New Market road, and Jackson was pressing hard on the rear by way of the Chickahominy and the White Oak Swamp. For tunately for the success of the retreat, Stuart's cavalry, owing to Lee's misapprehension of McClellan's movements after the battle of Gaines' Mill, was all on the north side of the Chickahominy, pressing Stoneman's cavalry toward White House, and thus the march along the narrow blockaded roads of the swamp was not impeded. Heintzelman had crossed at Brackett's Ford on the evening of the 29th, and occupied the position on the southerly part of the great clearing called there Glendale, lately vacated by Porter's corps, which had followed Keyes toward the James. The cleared tract near White Oak Bridge was held by Franklin.

On the morning of June 30th, by order of the General-in-Chief, Franklin posted Slocum's division on the right of the Charles City cross-roads. The divisions of Smith and Richardson, together with that of Naglee, who had been put under General Franklin's orders, were stationed in the woods in a position to command the White Oak Swamp bridge. The artillery of the Second Division, commanded by Captain R. B. Ayres, Fifth Artillery, composed of his own, Mott's, and Wheeler's batteries—the latter so reduced that he had but two guns available for service—was placed in position to cover the crossing. About noon the enemy opened so heavy a fire upon this position, that the artillery was compelled to withdraw, abandoning one gun of Mott's battery—which was left on the field—in direct disobedience of Ayres' orders. It was from this direction that Jackson was approaching, and the furious fire of artillery opened on Franklin was from a battery of 28 guns, posted under cover on the north side of the swamp, which compelled the Union batteries to retire. A cavalry force took advantage of this to cross the creek, but was soon driven back. Wooding's battery, of Jackson's corps, was unable to keep its position in face of the fire of the Union sharpshooters; and Jackson, finding that the crossing was controlled by our fire, bivouacked that night in hearing of the heavy firing at Glendale, which told him that Longstreet's men were engaged; but the character of the soil, the destruction of the bridge over the marsh and creek, and the strong position of our troops prevented his advance until the following morning. After our troops retired, the bridge was rebuilt, and Jackson pressed on in pursuit.*

BATTLE OF GLENDALE, OR NELSON'S FARM.

Longstreet and A. P. Hill, as soon as they were informed of the direction of McClellan's retreat, in pursuance of Lee's orders crossed the New Bridge, and moved by the Darbytown road to the Long Bridge road, and came upon our men strongly posted across the Long Bridge road, about a mile from its intersection with the Charles City road, on June 30th. By order of General McClellan, McCall's division halted on the New Market road, near where it turns off to Quaker Church, with Meade's brigade on the right, Seymour's on the left, and Reynolds' (captured at Gaines' Mill) in command of Colonel Simmons, Fifth Pennsylvania, in reserve, Randol's regular battery on the right and front, Kerns' and Cooper's in the centre, and Dietrich's and Knierim's batteries of the reserve artillery all in front of the infantry line. Slocum's line, composed of Generals Newton's, Taylor's, and Bartlett's brigades, extended to the right from Charles City road. He had with him Upton's, Porter's, and Hexamer's batteries. General Kearney's division was posted so as to guard the space between the Charles City and the New Market roads, Robinson on the left supporting Thompson's battery, General Birney on his right, and General Berry in reserve. General McCall was on Kearney's left and front.

---

* Jackson's Report, iv., p. 42.

Hooker's division of Heintzelman's corps on the right of Sumner's corps, with Thompson's and Kirby's batteries, were in the rear of McCall's line, which was formed with the left refused. This irregular formation of the line of battle was in part due to the irregularities of the ground and the thick woods. The line of battle not being perfectly true, the artillery of the several divisions was in position in most cases in front of the covering infantry. The attack began about 2.30 P.M., in great force, and with furious violence, and was directed mainly against General McCall, whose division suffered so severely at Gaines' Mills, and which now numbered but 6,000 men.

The battle began on his front at 2.30 o'clock P.M., and soon after 3 P.M. his left was threatened by a heavy column of the enemy which passed through the woods and fell upon General Seymour, who was promptly reinforced by Colonel Simmons, sent to his aid by General McCall just in time to repel a furious attack with infantry and artillery on that flank; the fight lasted here for about two hours, when the enemy retired. The two German batteries, Diedrich's and Knierim's, were driven to the rear. General McCall sent them back to their position, but with little avail—as the guns were soon after abandoned by the cannoneers.

Six companies of the Twelfth Pennsylvania Regiment, Colonel Taggart, had been posted at two log-houses and breastwork of logs two hundred yards in advance of the extreme left of the Third Brigade, and the remaining four companies of the regiment were posted to cover two pieces of artillery on a hill in rear of the regiment. The enemy advanced in heavy columns from the road in front and opened with artillery on the six companies. These, seeing themselves in danger of being cut off by a party advancing up a ravine to their rear, broke and fled; the remainder supporting the two-gun battery was also driven back. The regiment did not appear on the field again that day as an organized body. The fugitives from this part of Seymour's line are those referred to in Hooker's report (p. 490) as rushing down the road and over the fields, breaking through his lines and firing on his men as they passed. Colonel Taggart gives his loss in this action as 6 killed, 36 wounded, and 23 missing.

Meantime a steady pressure had been kept up along the whole of McCall's line.

In the charges of the enemy which were repulsed three stand of colors were captured; one by Private W. F. Gallagher, of the Ninth Regiment, who killed the rebel color-bearer in a bayonet charge. The Third and Tenth charged a rebel battery and routed its infantry support, capturing 100 prisoners, but being suddenly assailed by a large force of the enemy were forced to retire, bringing their prisoners with them. The six companies of the Twelfth Regiment which had been sent to the support of General Seymour, and detached from the line by this countercharge of the rebels, were cut off, and at the same moment the section of a "Dutch" battery belonging to Porter was abandoned by the artillerymen, who cut loose their horses and broke through the cavalry and the infantry, bringing the prisoners to the rear. This separation of the Twelfth Regiment General McCall considers the one injudicious or unfortunate movement on his part of the line during the day.

Soon after this a charge was made on Randol's battery of a peculiar and most determined character. A brigade of rebels in wedge shape, without order, trailing arms, made a dash at the battery. Like charges by single regiments had been previously repulsed by the artillery, and in this instance so confident was Captain Randol of his ability to hold the ground that the Fourth Regiment was requested to withhold its fire. The guns tore great gaps in the advancing host, but the gaps were closed up, the mass moved on swiftly, steadily, with wild yells. Before its momentum could be checked or the guns limbered up it was upon them, among them, over them; the limbered guns were overturned, the horses killed, and the great surge of rebels sweeping onward drove all of the Fourth Regiment, except Company B, before it. This company, with men of other commands, stood their ground, and presented a brave front. General McCall rode in among the men, endeavoring to rally them, with partial success. A fierce bayonet fight under his own eye followed—it was a melee in which point or butt was used; the gallant company was carried to the rear surrounded by the yelling rebels, who were so intent on pursuing those in front that they walked through a gap in a fence which they passed, and escaped capture. McCall's right was now broken, and his entire line borne to the rear, with the loss of some guns. Falling back with two men of his cavalry escort, General McCall about two hundred yards in rear of his own line came upon two regiments of Berry's brigade, Kearney's division. Shortly after, General Kearney came up and formed two lines in the wood on the right of the road, saying as he did so, "If you (General McCall) can bring on another line in a few minutes I think we can stop them," and in the gathering darkness General McCall rode forward for this purpose, but fell into the lines of the Forty-seventh Virginia, by whom he was taken prisoner. General Kearney took measures at once to fill up the break in the line caused by the defeat of McCall. He posted the First New Jersey Brigade in that place and moved forward to where General Caldwell was putting two regiments into line on the right of the road, a quarter of a mile in the rear of breastworks then unoccupied, toward which the rebel skirmishers were distrustfully approaching. Kearney led a regiment to take possession of this work, and these misapprehending orders, fired at the rebels and at a part of Kearney's line; thus, while the rebels were driven off, for a time our own men were firing into each other, and in this fire General Kearney supposed, and so reported, General McCall as killed.

This attack at 4 P.M. struck Kearney also, and he states in his report that he was astonished at the vigor and determination of the assault in mass on his line. The slightly sloping ground in his front was swept by the fire of Thompson's battery, with such execution upon the advancing host that they were mowed down by ranks. The survivors halted for a moment, the gaps were filled, and the wave swept on, across the open ground in Kearney's front, advancing at a run over the two hundred paces which separated the hostile forces. Notwithstanding the loss caused in their heavy masses by this terrible fire, they still pressed on with a fortitude and persistency that, as Kearney says, put artillery out of the "calculation." Then the Sixty-third Pennsylvania, Colonel Hayes, and half the Thirty-seventh New York Volunteers moved up to the line of the guns and charged the enemy and opened on them such rapid and well-sustained volleys that what grape and canister had failed to accomplish, musketry effected. The artillery recommenced its fire; three times during the afternoon was this advance on the guns repeated, and as often was it driven back.

About the time General McCall's division gave way, General Heintzelman had become assured that the attack on the Charles City road was not the serious one, and rode over to General Sumner's headquarters in front of Nelson's farmhouse, to make preparations to meet the enemy who had turned the left. De Russy's battery, with several other batteries which were already put in position, were firing over the heads of the retreating troops. General Burns' brigade was advanced to meet the enemy and it soon drove them back. At this time the troops from White Oak Swamp were coming on the field, and Heintzelman, knowing that Sumner's troops were all engaged, sent General Slocum's New Jersey brigade, under General Taylor, with a battery to General Kearney, who had called for aid. These soon drove back the enemy. Heintzelman rode out on the Charles City road far enough to learn that there was nothing to fear from the enemy in that quarter. He apprehended that they might bring up fresh men against our worn-out ones, and learning that General Franklin's men had already begun the retreat, arrangements were speedily made for the whole force to follow, which it did. Heintzelman reached headquarters at 1.30 A.M., and soon after daylight his divisions were in position on Malvern Hill.

General Sumner receiving intelligence that General Franklin had retreated and that General Heintzelman was about to do so, at 9 P.M. fell back with reluctance. He knew he had won a victory and did not wish to leave the field. The object of the rebels in this attack on the retreating column was to cut it in two at the Charles City crossroads and gain possession of the Quaker road. Had this attempt been successful, or had they been able to detain the Union troops long enough to enable Jackson to gain the rear at White Oak Swamp, the result might have been disastrous. As it was, they were baffled in their attempts either to break our line or delay the march. Franklin kept Jackson at bay and prevented him from crossing at White Oak Bridge, while Sumner and Heintzelman with Slocum and McCall repulsed the attacks of Longstreet and Hill. The only reverse suffered was that on McCall's line, where we

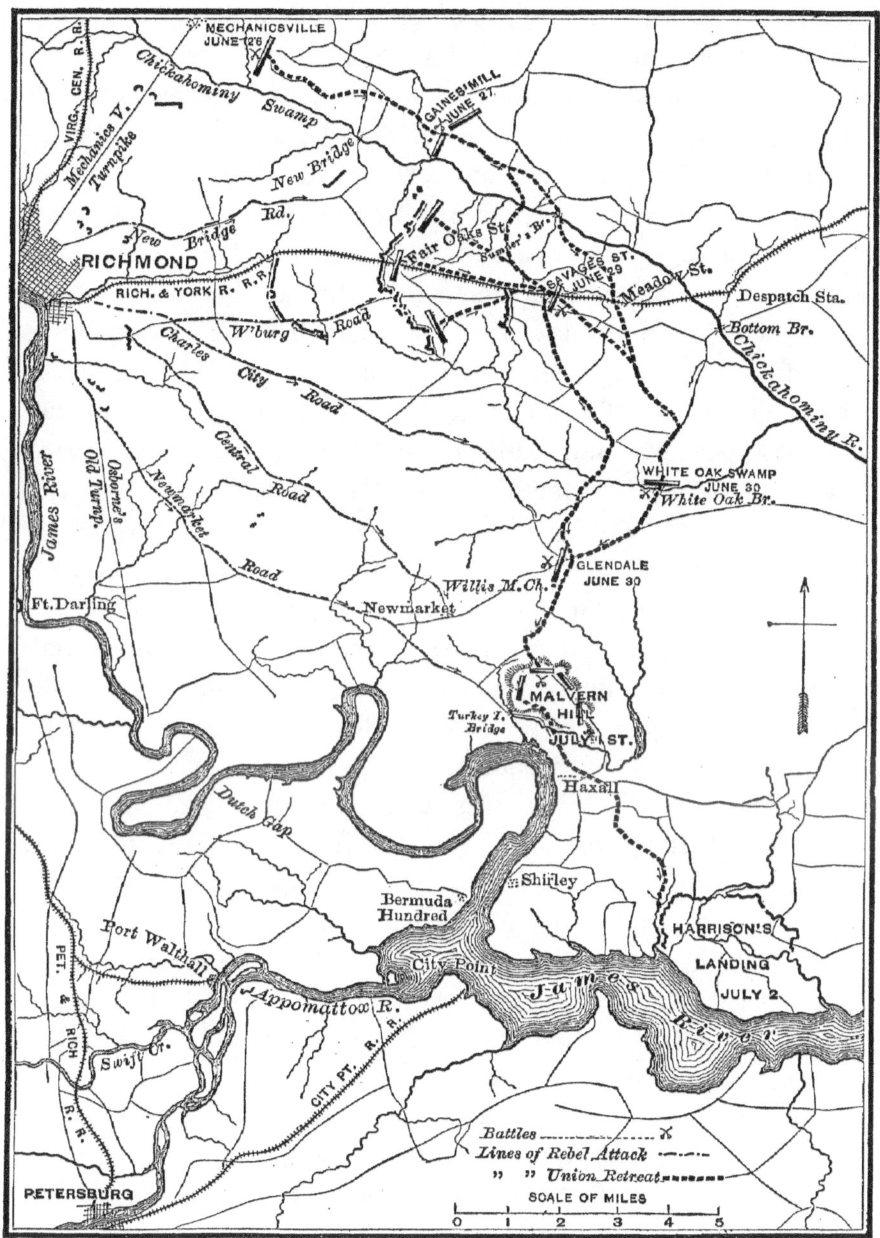

Field of the "Seven Days'" Battle.

lost ten pieces of artillery, and some of these were abandoned on the field and not secured by the enemy until the next day. The retreat was resumed at night, and by morning of the next day all were posted on the slopes of Malvern Hill. The rebels did not make any extravagant claims to success. Longstreet says: "Owing to the nature of the ground—that concert of action so essential to complete success could not obtain—particularly attacking such odds against us in position. The enemy, however, was driven back slowly and steadily, contesting the ground inch by inch. He succeeded in getting some of his batteries off the field and, by holding his last position until dark, in withdrawing his forces under cover of night." General A. P. Hill states: "The charge which broke McCall's line was made by Field and Pender's divisions; the Sixtieth and Fifty-fifth Virginia captured two batteries of Napoleon guns, and the Sixtieth crossed bayonets with the enemy, who obstinately contested their possession. About dark the enemy pressed us so hard along the whole line—that my last reserve was directed to advance cautiously: it seemed that a tremendous effort was being made to turn the fortune of the battle. The volume of fire that, approaching, rolled along the line, was terrific; in five minutes all firing ceased."

Longstreet reports his loss from June 27th to 30th, aggregate, 4,429; A. P. Hill from June 26th to 30th, aggregate, 4,074; D. Hill, aggregate, 3,955, Total, 12,458. Hill captured 14 guns and two stand of colors. In all this there is nothing of the exultation of victory.

General George G. Meade, afterward famous as the Commander-in-chief of the Army of the Potomac in the battle of Gettysburg, was badly wounded at this battle and was obliged to retire from the field.

On this date also, the 30th, still another affair occurred

which calls for a brief reference. While one part of the army was holding Jackson in check at White Oak Bridge, and another saved our line of retreat at Glendale, a portion of Hunt's reserve artillery, supported by Sykes' regulars, prevented a third body of rebels from intercepting our march.

General Sykes reached the plateau of Malvern Hill about 11 o'clock A.M. on the 30th, where, by order of General Porter, the artillery was posted so as to control the approaches in front. Part of Colonel Buchanan's brigade was on the right in a pine grove, the other two regiments in support of Weed's regular battery, the Tenth Infantry, Major Lovell, to the left, covering the regular batteries of Edwards, Carlisle, and Smead, and a New York battery of the reserve. Warren's brigade on the extreme left covered the river road to Richmond, supported by the Eleventh Infantry and Martin's battery of Napoleon guns, and a detachment of cavalry for outpost duty. Sykes says, "Nothing could be more commanding than the line I held." The rebel Generals Holmes and Wise, in the afternoon saw the troops moving along the Quaker road, as they say in their reports, in great haste and disorder toward Malvern Hill, and, feeling strong with their detachment of 7,000 men and 6 batteries, were eager to attack. They pushed down the river road, where they met General Lee, and by his advice put their infantry into position to support their guns, of which they had sent forward six rifled pieces to within eight hundred yards of Malvern Cliff, that being the name given by them to this affair. Before they could get their guns to work, they were astonished to find our troops opening on them from the hill with twenty-five or thirty pieces, while a gunboat in the river began dropping huge shells among the infantry supports. Their battery of six rifles was destroyed, two caissons were blown up, and the artillerists and some cavalry rushed in wild flight to the rear, riding over the infantry, who were not slow to follow the example set them. General Holmes declared that to attack an enemy so strongly posted would be madness, in which opinion General Wise concurred, and they retired, to take no part even in the battle of the following day.

Thus the Union troops had successfully resisted three separate attacks on flank and rear on this eventful 30th of June. There was no more critical day in the campaign; and that the crisis was safely passed was due mainly to the courage and discipline of our men, and the alertness and skill of corps, division, and brigade commanders, whose best energies were exerted to take the army intact to the James.

It now remains to notice the closing scenes of the campaign.

CHAPTER VIII.

BATTLE OF MALVERN HILL.

IT will be remembered that, by orders of the Commander-in-Chief, General Keyes had crossed White Oak Swamp with his corps, and on the afternoon of the 29th had put the trains in motion from Turkey Bridge for the James River. He had become familiar with this region through scouting parties of the Eighth Illinois and Eighth Pennsylvania Cavalry. Captain Kernan, of the latter regiment, an excellent officer, and as skilful as an Indian in woodcraft, who lost his life in a grand charge which stayed the rush of Jackson's men on the Eleventh Corps at Chancellorsville, in 1863, is mentioned by Keyes as of special aid to him in finding out the roads in this unknown region. Fitz John Porter's corps was in support of Keyes, and both were ordered to occupy a position resting on the James, at or near Turkey Bend, perpendicular to the river and covering Charles City road, and to open communication with the gunboats, while the wagon-train was pushed on to Haxall's and Harrison's plantations. Harrison's Landing was afterward selected as the base by General McClellan, after consultation with Commodore Rodgers on board the gunboat Galena, as from that position better protection could be given to the camps by the fire of the gunboats.

After the close of the several engagements on the 30th, the whole army was put in position on Malvern Hill.

Malvern Hill is an eminence near the north or left bank of the James River, sixty feet in height, its summit presenting an open plateau of some extent. It rises somewhat abruptly at its northern side, and on the south and east is guarded by Western River and thick underwood; its western edge is also protected by forests and swamp, difficult for horse or artillery. Between the two rivers is the approach to the northern front, up which the Quaker road passes, in front of the Crew house, where it divides. The western foot of the hill is traversed by the New Market road. The slopes of the hill formed an admirable position to post or manœuvre troops; and either flank, if threatened, could be supported across the plateau on the top. General McClellan had given orders for placing the troops, before they had all arrived upon the spot, and had assigned positions to Porter's corps and Couch's division of Keyes'; the other corps, as they came on the ground, were put in position by General A. A. Humphreys, who had examined the ground thoroughly the day before. The army was disposed in the form of a huge semicircle, its wings resting on the river, with the right at Haxall, where it was protected by the fire of the gunboats. General Morell was posted on the extreme left, with his headquarters at the Crew house, the brigade of Griffin in advance; Martindale's brigade in the Crew field immediately north of the Richmond road, Butterfield's in its rear on the south side of the Richmond road, both in close order, the men lying down, and ready to support Griffin's brigade or meet an attack on the left. General Griffin had command of all the artillery on the left, and Colonel McQuade's Fourteenth New York Volunteers, with a section of Weeden's battery, was watching that flank. Buchanan's and Lovell's brigades of Sykes' division was near and in rear of Morell, Warren's brigade having been thrown into the valley below the plateau, watching the river road. McCall's division was in rear of Porter and Couch. Couch's division, with its left near Morell, was deployed half way to the woods at the foot of the hill, its right on a ravine, which extended almost as far as the West house, and separated the left from the centre; Heintzelman, from the ravine to the wood at the West house in the centre, across the Quaker road, Kearney on the left, Hooker on the right. Between Hooker and the Binford house was Sumner's corps, prolonged until it met the divisions of Smith and Slocum, of Franklin's corps. The bridge at Carter's Mill and the approach to Haxall's, where several roads converge, were guarded by Keyes, with Peck's division. The position was most favorable for the use of cannon. The reserve artillery, under General Hunt, was posted by that able officer on the height on the west of the plateau and in front of the brick house. Batteries of 20- and 32-pounders, with rifled and Napoleon guns, formed a terrible array; below them were the infantry awaiting attack with firm confidence. Sixty pieces had a converging fire from Porter's line, and all along the crest of the hill, wherever one was needed, a battery made its appearance at the moment. Those who had toiled to drag the guns across the swamp and up the hill were rewarded for their labor—the First Connecticut Heavy Artillery distinguishing itself among volunteers in this branch of the service.*

The artillery reserve under General Hunt, with Colonels Wm. Hays and Getty as brigade commanders, together with the horse-batteries of Tidball, Benson, and Robertson, also contributed to the success of this movement to a degree which entitles them to a special mention in this connection.

On the right of General Couch's position, extending

*An examination of the reports of nearly all the Union generals discloses many details of Malvern Hill which cannot be introduced here for lack of space.

down toward the enemy, was a grove which General Humphreys desired to have slashed, that it might not afford a cover for attack; but he was unable to secure the men necessary for the work. Though a part of it nearest his lines was occupied by Couch, the enemy found opportunity to use it, but were driven out later in the day by Abercrombie, so that Couch was able to advance his line for some distance, so as to effectually command the ravine on his left. The foot of the hill was densely wooded; in front of Crew's house at the base of the hill, and one mile distant, about one hundred yards from the farm fence, was a deep ravine running parallel to it. Here Armistead's rebel brigade formed.

During the battle of Glendale, when McCall's division broke, many fugitives did not rejoin their command, but passed to the rear as rapidly as possible, joining the ever-increasing column that led the way to the river and the shelter of the gunboats. These cast away everything that might impede their flight, save their arms and ammunition, and while intent on safety, were not unprepared for resistance. When they reached a point from which the waters of the James were brought into view, and they saw the gunboats swinging at anchor, their spirits revived, discipline asserted its power, and they sought to join their commands. All through the long morning, dusty and powder-stained men in close column climbed the steep Quaker road, under direction of staff officers who had carefully examined the ground. In front of some parts of the line were slight trenches, barely deep enough to be called rifle-pits. Of entrenchments there were none; the crests and inequalities of the ground served as sufficient cover to the artillery, and the men below and between the guns looked out over the wide sweep of open ground between them and the forest which hid the enemy from view. From the Crew house McClellan could overlook the movements of the enemy, and see the divisions of Longstreet and Hill filing into position in the rear of Jackson. These troops had been so roughly handled the day before, and their numbers so diminished, that they required rest, and took no active part in the movements of the first day. Lee, whose army was as weary with the labor of the past week as our own, felt it a necessity incumbent upon him to attack, although he was urged by some of his best officers not to press McClellan further. He and his staff were more ignorant of the roads and the approaches to the hill than our own men, who had studied the topography of the region assiduously with a view to this movement. Magruder, for instance, who cannot be accused of lack of zeal in his cause, pressed forward to the Quaker road with his own division and that of the veteran General Huger; but both lost their way, and their failure to reach Glendale in time to take part was most disastrous to the rebels.

Lee marshalled his forces, Jackson's command with D. H. Hill on his right, Whiting on his left, with one of Ewell's brigades occupying the interval, the rest of Ewell's and Jackson's own division in reserve. Two of Huger's brigades were formed next to Hill; Magruder was on the right with his own and one of Huger's brigades. Ignorance of the country, the difficulty of communication, the density of the forests, which hindered the movement of artillery and made it impossible to bring up a sufficient force of that arm to oppose successfully the extraordinary strength in that regard opposed, are among the reasons advanced by General Lee why this final effort of his army was not a success. His report, and those of all the other rebel commanders who took part in the action, are meagre.

On the rebel side the orders were to advance at a given signal, which was to be a yell, cheer, or shout, to be uttered by Armistead's brigade as it took the lead. But Armistead's brigade was cut off by part of Huger's division and by Magruder's, and the sound of a shout when a shout was raised was not heard all along the line, being lost in the sound of the guns on the hill.

About 1 o'clock P.M. Whiting's and D. H. Hill's advance appeared in the plain beyond the belt of woods at the foot of the hill, and were immediately fired on by our artillery, which inflicted a heavy loss while they were crossing an open field and fording a stream to get under cover. Here they were halted for a while to examine the Union position. When the examination was completed, D. H. Hill was confirmed in his opinion, previously expressed, that the attack could not but be hazardous to their arms. While this portion of the rebel army was halting here, awaiting the proper disposition of their artillery, so as to distract and crush the fire of the Union guns, the division of General Hill was put in motion, that of General Whiting being held on the road near Poindexter's house, covering batteries which were exposed to a concentrated fire from the hill, and which were disabled and retired almost as fast as they were brought up, until the weight of the attack upon the left was developed, when these guns were turned so as to command the rebel approach.

During the whole morning there had been a constant artillery fire; occasionally small bodies of the enemy emerged from the woods and approached near enough to open musketry fire upon the gunners, but as often as they appeared the concentrated fire of four batteries drove them away with loss. In front of Couch this was repeated three times, twice on his right and once on his left; the last, at three o'clock, was made on Palmer and Abercrombie on the right of Couch, in which a stand of colors of the Fourteenth North Carolina, of

Anderson's brigade, was captured. The division of D. H. Hill waited for the signal. Huger and Magruder on his right did not wait. As soon as Magruder could get a battery in position he opened fire, and sent a regiment to charge up the hill in front on Couch's left. The battery was crushed by the fire brought on it, and the charging regiment hurled back with loss. Three times he tried the same experiment, and three times met with a like repulse. General Magruder's report is very like a romance; but bold as his final charge was, and far as it was pushed, his determined men were never near enough to threaten seriously the safety of the main Union batteries. Some of the field batteries which were in exposed positions were limbered up and withdrawn to more favorable ones, and again opened fire on his advance. As to the signal for the rebel attack, it is enough of a military curiosity to be given in full. It is appended to Magruder's report as Inclosure No. 5, July 1, 1862:

Batteries have been established to rake the enemy's line. If it is broken, as is probable, Armistead, who can witness the effect of the fire, has been ordered to charge with a yell. Do the same.

By order General Lee.

R. H. CHILTON,
Assistant Adjutant-General.

General Armistead, to whom the duty of shouting was prescribed, advanced three regiments to drive off some skirmishers, which he says were repulsed, but went so far that neither of them could either advance or recede. They were obliged to take advantage of an inequality of the ground and lie down to escape from the fire of the artillery. They were not relieved until after nightfall. Armistead also begged for more artillery, but failed to have his wants supplied, although Longstreet promised to do so. Magruder wanted thirty pieces of rifled artillery, but it did not come. D. H. Hill sent Jackson a message stating that the fire of isolated batteries was worse than useless, only exposing the batteries to be destroyed in detail, and insisted that one hundred guns should be concentrated upon the Union line. Jackson replied by repeating the order to advance at the signal. Later in the afternoon, about 5.30 o'clock, Hill heard the sound of loud shouting on his right, followed by heavy musketry fire; this he supposed to be the appointed signal, and gave orders for his men to advance. Garland in front attacked the hill with impetuous courage, but soon sent for reinforcements. The Sixth Georgia, and the brigade of General Toombs, which was under partial shelter in the rear, were sent to his assistance. General Hill in person accompanied the column. They approached the crest in handsome order, but discipline was of no avail to hold them there, much less to make them advance farther. They soon retreated in disorder. Gordon, commanding Rhodes' brigade, had made a gallant advance and some progress, as had also Ripley and Colquitt's and Anderson's brigades; all these were now streaming wildly to the rear. Heedless of command and deaf to entreaty they sought the woods near Willis church on the Quaker road. Ransom's brigade of Huger's division was sent to the aid of Hill, but these manifested no eagerness to tempt fate in front of those batteries. Winder, of Jackson's division, and later Early came to the rescue, but both these brigades were soon huddled together with the same disorganized mass of troops. They suffered from the fire, but accomplished nothing. A careful reading of D. H. Hill's report of his part of the battle, shows plainly the loss and demoralization of his division, and gives a glimpse of the disorder hidden by the woods about the little parsonage.

No more positive admission of defeat with loss and disorder can be looked for. Hill upbraids everybody, from the Commander-in-Chief down to Whiting and Holmes, whom he asserts were not engaged at all. He complains of want of concert and unity of action, and is eager to assert and probably believes that he did, as he says, engage the whole "Yankee" force with his single division.

The plain truth is Hill attacked on Couch's right. What he describes as the breaking and retreat of the whole line was only that of some of Sedgwick's men, who had been sent to act as supports when the attack was heaviest, changing places with those of the infantry in front of the line whose cartridge-boxes were empty, that they might go to the rear and replenish—a movement which was made in good order without confusion, and which no doubt tended to accelerate the withdrawal of Hill's men to the grove about the parsonage. He further says that, so far as he can learn, no one of the rebels drew trigger except McLaw's division, his own, and a part of Huger's. His report is dated——— 1862, and written, as it must have been, long after the battle. Hill betrays at least great ignorance of the actions of his brother officers. Nevertheless it is true that the rebel force was not handled as a whole in concert of action. After giving the final orders for battle, General Lee apparently left the execution to the division commanders. The signal for onset was inadequate for fighting in thick woods. But while there was a want of absolute coincidence in the movements of the rebel generals, Hill is inaccurate in saying that there was no attack made at the same time as his own. Magruder had placed his three divisions on the right of Huger's *en echelon* to the right and rear. Magruder, who was ordered to support Armistead, went forward to reconnoitre the position. He found part of Armistead's brigade in line of battle under the brow of a wooded hill, along the crown of which passed a road which was parallel to a field occupied by the Union troops. Here he selected his own line, taking the road as a good position on which to form troops.

The field in which the batteries nearest to him were placed was the Crew farm, and the nearest and best line was that which led up to it from the meadow on the extreme right of his line, where the advance would be in a measure protected by the natural cover of the hill. Crew's house was the key to the position; about it were grouped the heavy siege-guns, while battery above battery, with long lines of infantry, sometimes protected by slashing and sometimes by rifle pits, which Kearney had dug in front of his division, held the salient points of the position. As Magruder got his men in place, the fire from these batteries became, as stated, intense. His plan was to put 15,000 men in line and charge the batteries and supporting infantry, to follow up success with fresh troops, and if repulsed to hold the line where he then was on the hill. His caution as to repulse was one that did credit to his military sagacity and was fully justified by events.

Although the batteries were not carried, the assault contributed much to the rout, panic, and demoralization which marked the enemy's escape from the field early in the night. Darkness set in and he concluded to let the battle subside and occupy the field; pickets were set and a part of Armistead's brigade encamped within one hundred yards of the Union guns. Lee is satisfied that the Union loss was far greater than his own, and winds up with the remark that there was no attack so far as he knows by General Holmes on his right. Holmes and Huger seem to be impediments in the way of the rebel commanders in this campaign, and are made the scapegoats of rebel reports. Having seen what General Magruder claims, let us look further at what he did on the field.

About the same time that D. H. Hill advanced to make his attack—say about 5.30 P.M.—Magruder, who waited in vain for the thirty pieces of rifled artillery for which he had sent to silence the Union fire, became impatient at the delay, and ordered General Armistead's brigade to advance, and at the same time put his own division in motion. He sent forward Wright's brigade first, Mahone's next, substituted three regiments of Cobb's for the remainder of Armistead's raw troops, sent in General Ransom to his left, in person superintended the advance of Barksdale's brigade of his own division, and sent staff officers in quick succession to urge an attack by Huger on his left. As they emerged from the cover of the woods in which their line was formed and breasted the slope of the hill, now swept by the converging fire of the heavy batteries at the Crew house, the advance was checked, but they were easily rallied and led again with fury to the attack; but the line made no further progress, even in Magruder's report. Ransom and Jones, with the remainder of Armistead's men, were urged forward to the support of their faltering comrades. McLaw's division was also sent in by order of General Lee, and Magruder was urged to press the enemy on the right. They advanced bravely all along the line, but only to recoil before the storm of missiles which each fresh effort on their part drew from the heavy guns. The day was drawing to an end and Magruder gave his attention to securing the ravine and woods where he had formed his line, and to procuring reinforcements to guard against any reverse. All the rebel generals ascribe their failure to reach the hill to the preponderance of the artillery fire on the

Union side, their own inefficiency in that arm, and to want of support and co-operation in attack. In truth there seem to have been few orders issued on the 1st by the rebel general-in-chief.

Magruder claims to have had under his command that day between twenty-six and twenty-eight thousand men, and estimates his loss at 2,900, and that of the Union troops at 6,000 or 7,000 from his fire alone!

The battle began by an advance against Porter's and Couch's position on the left and centre of the line by an advance by skirmishers which drove in Berdan's sharpshooters. The rebels were speedily repulsed by artillery alone. Along other parts of the line there was a desultory artillery fire kept up with no material result, save the annoyance it caused to the men who were under fire and obliged to be passive. On the extreme right Smith and Slocum of Franklin's corps were not engaged during the day. Between the left of Smith and the right of Sumner was a point which was deemed weak, as it was here that the main road from the crossing at White Oak Swamp came in; near the mill pond on Smith's right the trees had been slashed by Duane, of the Engineers, by order of General Humphreys, who remained on the front of Sumner and Heintzelman during the greater part of the day, as there were indications of an attack in that quarter, but no attempt was made here save a slight one on Sumner's right, of which that General made no report, as he says that during the action the commanding general came on the field and he (Sumner) ceased to command.

The weight of the battle, it will be seen, fell upon Morell of Porter's corps, and Couch of Keyes'. About 3 P.M., Anderson, of D. H. Hill's division, charged against the right of Couch and became engaged with Palmer's* Brigade. They were met by a sharp musketry fire, and as soon as a battery

* Late Devin's.

could be brought to bear were put to rout, leaving the flag of the Fourteenth N. Carolina in the possession of the Thirty-sixth New York Regiment. An assault, which was made by a part of D. H. Hill's division, spread along the centre, also involving the left of Heintzelman, and was speedily repulsed. The ravine between Couch's right and the left of Heintzelman, a point which invited attack, was held by a strong detachment from Palmer's and Birney's brigades, which were protected by intrenchments along their front. In the furious assault made on this portion of the line later in the day these regiments assisted in repulsing the enemy.

There are discrepancies as to the time at which the most fiercely contested encounters of the day took place. D. H. Hill gives the hour of his order to advance as about one and a half hour before sunset; Magruder that of his at 5.30 P.M.; Couch says that about 4.30 P.M. the enemy rapidly pushed forward a heavy column into the open field and advanced boldly from their right and opened the attack upon Griffin, of Morell's division, whose front was protected by fourteen rifled Parrott guns, and eleven field pieces, supported by the Fourth Michigan, Ninth Massachusetts, and Sixty-second Pennsylvania. Here was the pinch of this fight. The enemy advanced steadily until it came within range of the rifled guns, when it was stopped and formed line. Kingsbury's battery of six Parrott guns, having exhausted its ammunition, was withdrawn, and three guns of Battery C, Rhode Island Artillery, and two of the Fifth Massachusetts substituted.

This is the last effort of D. H. Hill's left, and the next scene in the drama is the charge of Magruder, the most famous of any made that day, already described.

As the efforts of Hill's men relaxed, there was still a heavy cannonade kept up by the rebels. Porter, who had fathomed the design of the enemy, husbanded his ammunition and reserved his musketry fire. His men were for the most part protected by the inequalities of the ground, by slight trenches and rifle pits in their front, and suffered comparatively little from the rebel fire. As soon as any man was wounded, he walked if able, or if not, was carried to the shelter of a bank in the rear, chosen as a temporary hospital; the bearers returned quietly and promptly to their places in the ranks.

In Morell's division they were disposed: Martindale in the centre, lying down, Griffin in front, Butterfield in the rear. The force of the final assault, for the first time that day, aroused the infantry into vigorous action along that part of the line, from Sykes' right to Heintzelman's left. The advancing rebel columns rushed forward upon the infantry line, which rose up to repel the onset. Morell was advised that a strong body of the enemy were availing themselves of the natural advantages to push up a valley upon his left and rear. Arrangements were promptly made to meet him, and were hardly completed when he appeared ascending the hill near the Crew house, and was promptly met by the Fourteenth New York, and after three attacks was driven off and did not renew his attempt in that quarter. At the same time a determined and powerful attack was made upon Morell's left front; the first assault was repulsed, but the enemy's line being constantly reinforced, the regiments which had advanced to support the batteries soon found their ammunition exhausted. These were regularly relieved by other regiments, who continued the conflict against superior numbers until these in turn were relieved by part of Sykes' division and Meagher's brigade of Richardson's, who came on the field led by General Porter in person.

In front of Couch's line was a like desperate encounter,

marked by the violence of the assault and the steady tenacity of the resistance by which it was met and repelled. The enemy made repeated efforts to drive in his right. If but once the rebels could only pierce that line and get among the guns which had held them at bay so long, the Union centre was parted, the army cut in two. But if Magruder saw the importance of the position, so did the Union commanders. Sumner, prompt to divine the place of danger, sent Caldwell's brigade, which went promptly into action. Heintzelman sent Seely's battery, which, under De Russy, Chief of Artillery, was put in position in front of Howe, and did its duty well. Sickles, with three regiments from Hooker's division, took an effective part, relieving some of the regiments whose ammunition was exhausted.

The struggle continued until nine o'clock P.M., when the rebels withdrew. The author, as an eye-witness, can assert that never for one instant was the Union line broken or their guns in danger. During the night the troops were withdrawn from the hill and put in motion toward Harrison's landing, seven miles distant, the Navy Department having decided that, owing to the narrowness of the James in the vicinity, it would be impossible for it to cover the transports and supplies against attack from the opposite bank. The post at Harrison's Landing was shelled by Stuart, who had been a week on his chase after Stoneman, but before Jackson, whom Stuart had notified of the opportunity, could come up to hold the hill (Evlington Heights), which commanded our camp, Stuart was driven off. The camp was afterward bombarded by the rebels from the opposite side of the James. They fired from heavy rifled guns and withdrew at daylight. This position was also occupied to guard against a repetition of the attempt.

Thus ended the first advance upon Richmond.

CHAPTER IX.

TERMINATION OF THE CAMPAIGN.

IF, in reviewing the history of the Army of the Potomac as narrated in the foregoing chapters, we are to derive any great lessons from our experience, it must obviously be from a study of the events of the entire twelve months, rather than from the isolated engagements. In giving opinions in regard to the plans and movements, we have been governed by the documentary evidence now brought before us by both sides. We have not differed very much from the criticisms of abler writers, who came to the same conclusions years ago without the use of these documents. We only confirm their views.

General McClellan was correct in his declaration, made to the Secretary of War, in October, 1861, that the object of the Government should be to "crush the army under Johnston, at Manassas." We believe that he could have done this, and that he failed because he overestimated the strength of the enemy's forces, and underestimated the fighting qualities of his own army. He had made a plan which required that he should move from Washington with 140,000 men, and still leave the city secure. From the moment it was thought that he was determined to abide by his demand for this large body of men with which to take the field, and he was considered unmindful of the requirements of the political situation, the active hostility of the strongest friends and advisers of the Administration was aroused. These men considered a forward movement of the Army of the Potomac a political necessity, and demanded it.

Centreville should have been retaken when Johnston held it with but 47,000 men. At that period General McClellan had 180,000 men. President Lincoln felt this, and the people were with him, when, relying on his instincts solely, he demanded "action." All the so-called interference, all the real interference with General McClellan's plans—all the want of confidence in his ability as the leader of an active army—all the want of faith in his intentions to fully support the views of the Government in regard to the objects of the war, and as to the means to carry them out, arose from the belief that in and about General McClellan's headquarters there was a lack of faith in the Government itself and of sympathy with the Administration. McClellan proceeded to create, equip and discipline the Army of the Potomac with a skill and persistency which will be the admiration of military students for all times. He inspired the army with confidence; it believed him to be right in all his measures, because it loved and respected him, and because he was its appointed leader and guide. It was prepared to do whatever he demanded. He did not display the dash and brilliancy necessary to obtain from it the best service of which it was capable, but he still commanded its implicit confidence. The Army of the Potomac never lost the reputation of being the best disciplined, best equipped, and most efficient army on this continent; and this reputation was due solely to General McClellan's system of organization.

The more prominent of the lessons of our experiences of these three months worthy of the study and discussion of military men, are based upon the following general statements of the main facts which relate to the strategy and movements of that period.

Manassas was not taken, but was abandoned by Johnston when he heard of the order of the President requiring the Assistant Secretary of War to provide the necessary transportation to move the Army of the Potomac to the lower Chesapeake. What had we done to force this evacuation of a position which had been held by the rebels in sight of the dome of the Capitol for eight long months? Nothing but to build up an army many times as strong as that of our foes. Not a single effectual reconnoissance, not a successful attempt to discover the actual strength of the rebels, had been made; yet General McClellan had confidence in his own plans. He believed that in the end he would be proved to be right, if his own propositions were kept secret and carried out; but still the Potomac was blockaded for months, Norfolk was used to build Merrimacs, and gunboats, and we remained in front of Washington, growing ourselves and watching the rebel forces grow, until we saw the latter fold their tents and steal away, having done all that they expected to do—having been able to keep us about Washington until they became able to meet us upon other battle-fields.

Read the letter of Admiral Goldsborough* upon the taking of Norfolk—take your map, place thereon Burnside's forces, Wool's force of 11,000 men, the Army of the Potomac and its detachments, and pause to wonder why we permitted

---

* INCLOSURE.

"NAVY DEPARTMENT, April 24, 1862.

"HON. E. M. STANTON, Secretary of War:

"SIR—I have the honor to transmit to you a copy of despatch No. 214 of Flag-Officer Goldsborough, received this day at this department. The views expressed by him in regard to the possession of Norfolk accord so fully with my own that I deem it a duty to communicate them to you. I know not that it is possible, in the existing state of things, to re-enforce General Burnside as proposed; but the

the James River to be lost to us, with such forces at our disposal.

How can we be less impatient than was our noble President at that hour? how less anxious and demonstrative than

---

capture of Norfolk would, in my opinion, next after New Orleans, be the most decisive blow that could be struck for the suppression of the rebellion.

"I also send you an extract from a despatch of Commander Missroon, of the steamer Wachusett, York River, in relation to the works of Yorktown.

"I am, very respectfully,
"Your obedient servant,
"GIDEON WELLES."

FIRST INCLOSURE.

"U. S. FLAG SHIP MINNESOTA,
"HAMPTON ROADS, April 22,1862.

"HON. GIDEON WELLES, Secretary of the Navy:

"SIR—Three white men—one of them accompanied by his wife and two children—were picked up last night by the Baltimore. They were in a boat, and had, as they say, escaped from Norfolk. One of them has been working for a long time past in the Gosport Navy Yard. He describes the Merrimac as being off the yard, with a large gang of men working upon her day and night, fitting shutters to all her side ports; she has always had them, he says, to her end ports. He also informs me that four new wooden gunboats have been completed at the Norfolk yard, and a fifth over in Norfolk, and that all are now ready for service. Furthermore, that at the Norfolk yard they are building rapidly a vessel to be just like the Merrimac in every respect, except in size, which is only to be about a thousand tons; that she is already far advanced toward completion in her wood-work, and has even the wood-work of her covering or house finished. Neither of her engines, nor any of her iron plates, have yet been put in place. It is expected that she will be ready for use in about a month or so. This, he says, is the only vessel to be plated that the enemy is preparing at Norfolk. Besides the above five gunboats, they are now building there four more.

" I am perfectly satisfied of the truth of all these statements.

"I am, respectfully,
"Your obedient servant,
"L. M. GOLDSBOROUGH .
"Flag-Officer commanding North Atlantic Blockading Squadron.

"N.B.—By a late Norfolk paper, which I forward to the department to-day, it appears that a fight came off last Friday, near Elizabeth City, between some of Gen. Burnside's men and the enemy, and that the latter were driven half way to Norfolk. The object of the attack on our part was, I know, to destroy the lock of the Dismal Swamp Canal at Sooth Mills, which I have no doubt has been accomplished effectually. With this lock destroyed and the Currituck link of the Albemarle and Chesapeake Canal kept choked, no iron-clad or other gunboats can go from Norfolk to the sounds of North Carolina. No vessel drawing over three, were the people shouting "On to Richmond." On to Richmond was only a phrase. Had we gone to Norfolk, that demand would have been satisfied. But a nation guided by minds capable of perceiving the main political benefits to be derived from the strife thrust upon us, was dissatisfied with the want of action on the part of the Army of the Potomac, and the people felt that the rebels grew faster in numbers and in confidence than did our own army, and through their representatives they demanded that the Army of the Potomac should try its strength with the rebels. The only man who did not seem to feel the full force of this public demand was the commander of the army himself.

At that moment, had he become more disposed to act than to secure his army from every possible chance of failure, he could have silenced all his enemies and have placed upon the shoulders of those who were antagonistic to him the full responsibility for any want of success which might have attended his movements. At this period General McClellan could have led the whole sentiment of the country, had he either moved on Manassas, had he cleared the lower Potomac of rebel batteries, or had he taken Norfolk.

---

or three and a half feet of water, can pass through Currituck Sound from Norfolk and so get into Croatan and Pamlico Sounds. I speak from positive information on this point, for I had the experiment tried in effect, by Lieut. Jeffers, when he was despatched by me in charge of an army stern-wheel boat, drawing only three feet or so of water, to destroy some salt-works at Old Currituck Inlet.

Could Gen. Burnside be promptly re-enforced with a body of 40,000 men, I am convinced that he could possess himself of Norfolk in a fortnight after their arrival at Roanoke Island. This idea I have entertained ever since that island surrendered to our arms, and the more I think of it, the more I am confirmed in my belief. With the force the General would then have, he would undoubtedly use the roads leading from Powell's Point, Winton, and Gatesville, all three of which are good and practicable, and hold Roanoke Island and Winton as bases of operation.

"These considerations may be of moment before a great while, if they are not so now.

"Most respectfully,

"L. M. G."

This is, then, to be the first deduction from the narrative of the events of 1861 and 1862: General McClellan did not give to the will of the President and the demands of the people that weight in the formation of his plans of campaign to which they were entitled.

When Johnston evacuated Manassas the rebels still held their position at Norfolk, thus securing to themselves a navy yard, and effectually blockading the James River against the navy and the United States transports. The Army of the Potomac was to be moved under new plans of campaign. General McClellan could no longer expect to surprise General Johnston, or cut his lines of communication with Richmond.

President Lincoln had assumed command of all the armies. To whom was he to turn for advice and assistance? To the general who had determined that all his plans as commander-in-chief, thus far ordered or submitted, were faulty?

President Lincoln was commander-in-chief, and as such, loved and respected by the whole people as a pure, earnest, honest ruler—brighter and quicker in perception of right and wrong than was any member of his cabinet. He knew the history of past wars. He shrank from no duty, but acted as his predecessors acted. He could not interfere; he could order, and he should have been obeyed. At least, the people and the army should never have known of any disagreements between him and the Commander of the Army of the Potomac.

From the records of the War Department we can determine the relative positions occupied by the President and the commanders of our armies during the War of 1812 and the Mexican War.

It appears that on November 25, 1846, the Secretary of

War wrote to General Taylor, in reply to the General's animadversions upon a despatch of the Secretary's in relation to the Tampico Expedition under General R. Patterson, as follows:

"You must be aware that in my official communications I am only the medium for presenting the views of the President, and you will not question his right, as Commander-in-chief, to make suggestions as to the movements of the forces under your command, or as to the officers to be employed in these movements. Having, in this instance, carefully qualified his suggestions so as to prevent them from being regarded as positive directions or commands, and expressly disclaimed the intention of employing any part of the troops which in your opinion 'would interfere with your operations,' he is entirely unconscious of having given any just cause for protest and complaint."

Again, on May 31, 1847, the Secretary of War reviews General Scott's action in not carrying out the instructions of the President respecting peace negotiations with which Mr. Trist was charged, and concludes as follows:

"Under these circumstances can you conceive that, as commanding general of the force in Mexico, you have the right to raise a question upon your duty to obey this direction, coming, as it does, through a proper channel from your superior, *the Commander-in-chief?* In my opinion you could not have wandered farther from the true view of the case than by supposing that the President or myself has placed you in a condition of deferring 'to the chief clerk of the Department of State the question of continuing or discontinuing hostilities.' I cannot conceive that any well-founded exception can be taken to the order you have received in relation to suspending hostilities, and I am fully persuaded that, if the contingency requiring you to act upon it shall ever occur, you will promptly carry it into full effect."

On June 15, 1847, the Secretary of War, referring to the same subject, and in reply to a letter from General Scott, says:

"In relation to the direction for an armistice or suspension of hostilities, the President, after duly considering all you have said on the subject, does not doubt that it was an order proper and right for him to give, and consequently one which you were bound to obey."

Judging from the actions of other Presidents, who, for reasons sound or otherwise, relieved other generals in command, President Lincoln should have relieved General McClellan, as was done on January 13, 1848, when the Secretary of War informed General Winfield Scott that the President had determined to relieve him from further duty as Commanding General in Mexico, and ordered that he turn over the command of the army to the senior officer present.

Wherein can we find a difference between the position of General McClellan with President Lincoln and that of the other generals who had commanded our armies, with their Presidents? None, except that General McClellan was nearer the President, and had greater facilities for explaining his plans and views to him. President Lincoln's orders and wishes should have been obeyed so far as it was in the power of the General commanding the Army of the Potomac to obey them, and the records do not show that any efforts were made to keep in accord with the President, or to prepare even for the carrying out of his plans, particularly that embracing an overland route to Richmond. No direct and earnest effort, such as the President had directed, was made. Nothing pointing toward a bold attack upon Johnston, or the turning of his position by the route chosen by the President, seemed to be even contemplated.

Thus was the confidence of the Government in General McClellan impaired, if not destroyed.

The Army left Washington for Fortress Monroe, to carry out a plan of campaign which we may describe as follows: The base was to be the Fortress; the James River was to be useless, being closed to us by the Merrimac. We were to move up the Peninsula, past Yorktown, and invest that place while McDowell was to invest and reduce Gloucester. We were then to make West Point the new base, and fight a battle between that point and Richmond. To do all this it was determined that we would require about 140,000 men.

This was the plan of General McClellan, with the base changed from Urbana, thus involving the siege and reduction of Yorktown and Gloucester, but still a proposition of his own.

The Warwick River was supposed to run from north to south; the road to Williamsburg from Newport News was supposed to run past Yorktown and not across the Warwick. No one thought of a line of works from Yorktown and down the Warwick, with its right on rebel gunboats. The Army of the Potomac was fairly bottled up unless it carried those works at Yorktown by coup-de-main, or seized Gloucester and forced the evacuation of Yorktown by running its batteries.

And now the salient features of the first and second plans of General McClellan became of vital importance. They are, in brief, the co-operation of the navy and the seizure of Gloucester by a large corps of the Army of the Potomac detailed for that purpose, and the holding of a force in the valley of the Shenandoah subject to the orders of the General himself.

General McClellan dismisses the subject with these few words:

"On my arrival at Fortress Monroe the James River was declared, by the naval authorities, closed to the operations of their vessels, by the combined influence of the enemy's batteries on its bank, and the Confederate steamers Merrimac, Yorktown, Jamestown, and Teazer.

"Flag-Officer Goldsborough, then in command of the United States squadron in Hampton Roads, regarded it (and, no doubt, justly) as his highest and most imperative duty to watch and neutralize the Merrimac, and, as he designed using his most powerful vessels in a contest with her, he did not feel able to detach for the assistance of the army a suitable force to attack the water-batteries at Yorktown and Gloucester. All this was contrary to what had been previously stated to me, and materially affected my plans.

"At no time during the operations against Yorktown was the navy prepared to lend us any material assistance in its reduction until our land batteries had partially silenced the works."*

At this point we must reiterate our assertion made in the body of this work: "Co-operation by the navy was not and could not have been secured at that date, *because Norfolk had not been taken* during the winter, as was urged by Admiral Goldsborough."

The Navy Department had not been impressed with the importance of this co-operation. Thus was the first step taken without proper provision for carrying out the main feature of a water approach to Richmond, as contrasted with the overland or direct route by Fredericksburg, which required no material aid from the navy. Truly was the Army of the Potomac in a false position.

What was to be done? Here was an army of invasion confronting a rebel line whose flanks rested on a fortified town and on gunboats, whose front was covered by a marsh, a river, and in large part by earthworks. Since McDowell's corps had been detained to defend Washington on the ground that General McClellan had disregarded the orders

* McC. Report, page 138. "I had no expectation of being relieved from the change of the operation in the Shenandoah Valley and in front of Washington, the President's War Order No.3 giving no intimation of such an intention; and that, so far as reference was made to final operation after driving Jackson back and taking such a position as to prevent his return, no positive order were given in the letter, the matter being left for future consideration when the proper time arrived for a decision."

of the President, and had not, in the opinions of Generals Hitchcock and L. Thomas, complied with the requirements of the recommendations of the council of war, no assault upon the works at Gloucester could be attempted with any probability of success.

The army found itself, immediately after the order which removed McDowell, in such a reduced state in point of numbers, and in such a false position in regard to the contemplated movement up the Peninsula, that it was absolutely imperative upon the Commanding General to do something to give spirit and morale to his troops, however hazardous such a course might appear to be. Thus, it was imperatively demanded of him to assault the rifle-pits in front of the enemy's centre at once. Here it was that General McClellan failed to seize upon the only opportunity then afforded him to place himself right before the nation. He should have then and there taken Yorktown. Desperate situations require desperate measures. We now know that he could have taken the place. But it seems to have been ordered otherwise.

An army not considered fit to assault new and not well-built field-works was to be used for a regular siege, ordinarily requiring a desperate final assault.

This was indeed a miserable plight in which to place an army of invasion. The Government (for it was not President Lincoln alone, but Secretaries Chase and Stanton, Generals Hitchcock and Thomas, and whoever else were in the secret councils)—the Government, we repeat, was responsible for this state of things. The greatest military error that could possibly have been committed was that which removed so important a corps from an army already in motion to carry out what was a well-digested plan.

It was the President's duty to secure Washington, if General McClellan had not done so already, but it never was his duty to strip General McClellan of a portion of his army in the field, in order to do this. He could not disregard the advice of those who counselled with him as military experts. It would have been better had he chosen men of more even temper and well-balanced mind. The resources of the country had not been drained—Washington was not in danger; if McClellan was active and the campaign in the Shenandoah had been under his direction, the works around Washington could have been held by bodies of militia alone. But, with blind indifference to whatever might result from it, these men persuaded the President to cripple the army sent out on a special mission, left the operations in the Shenandoah Valley under a thoroughly incompetent general, and in fact did everything to insure disaster to the Peninsula campaign.

Relieved from command of all the armies, fatally crippled after he was committed to the campaign up the Peninsula, General McClellan was fairly in the hands of those who had learned to distrust him and had become his adversaries.

Thus the army lay before Yorktown, prepared to consume weeks in conducting a siege against it. Encamped, and digging defences and approaches to field-works, the army was daily lowered in its own estimation by reading the mass of abuse which was found in the public press, and which was inspired by those principally active in the orders, recommendations, and investigations which led to this disastrous condition of affairs; abuse which was mostly personal and levelled against the commander who was directing the work. No wonder General Barnard is forced to say: "We did not carry away from Yorktown so good an army as we took there." Had General McClellan lost 6,000 men in making a single strong reconnoissance, no blame would have been attached to the attempt by the army or by the people. It was the only way out of the scrape, and we believe that upon the arrival of Smith, of Keyes' corps, with his division in front of Lee's Mills, the capture of the rebel breastworks was possible, the destruction of the rebel line and the capture of Yorktown following; and we now know that General Smith, upon his second reconnoissance on April 16th, proved that it was not impossible to force the rebel line at any period before that date.

The removal of McDowell's corps, we must again assert, was an act unworthy of any men pretending to be the military advisers of the President. They either knew nothing of the usual consequences of moving an army to attack the capital of a nation, or for partisan political purposes they were contented to advise the crippling of McClellan. They pretended not to know that the very reason they assigned for moving more troops to defend Washington would compel the rebels with their small force to keep all their troops to defend Richmond. No one then knew how little General McClellan was adapted to push matters after the armies had "locked horns"; the Government had the right to suppose that he needed but the opportunity, to attack with vigor, especially as the plan under which he was working was his own.

In the third chapter we have referred to the shrewdness of General Johnston in evacuating Yorktown as soon as he had become convinced that he delayed as long as prudence dictated. Had he remained, his army would have been captured.

General McClellan has been censured by many critics for remaining behind at Yorktown; but we must recall that it was known that the rebels intended to make the narrow portion of the Peninsula, near Williamsburg, their second line of defence to cover their retreat to Richmond. On page 74 of his report General McClellan writes: "It was also known that there were strong *defensive* works at or near Williamsburg."

Williamsburg is situated about one-third of the distance from Yorktown to the new base which was to be established by General McClellan at West Point, and from Yorktown to West Point is about thirty miles by water. It was not at all impossible, but, on the contrary, it was highly probable, that any strong corps sent by water to West Point, or to a point near it, would, under ordinary circumstances, completely cut off Johnston's retreat. It was therefore the duty of the Commanding General to urge on such troops as he intended should form this flanking column, which was to be under General Franklin. He had been distinctly informed by Chief Allen that, on May 3d, the rebels had had present in Yorktown from 100,000 to 120,000 men, and this chief had reported that he knew this because 119,000 rations had been issued. General McClellan had for the pursuit 109,335 men, and it was subsequently determined that the rebels withdrew from Yorktown with but 53,000 men. This false estimate of the rebel strength must always be an element in any discussion of the operations of the Army of the Potomac on the Peninsula.

This strange discrepancy between the actual numbers of the rebels at a given point and the number contained in General McClellan's despatches and official reports, wherever found, are all due to the gross miscalculations made by the Secret Service Division of the Army of the Potomac. Thus, March 8,1862, the rebel Army of the Potomac is stated to have been 150,000 strong, of which 80,000 were reported stationed at Centreville and vicinity; on March 11th there were only 47,000 men at that point. On March 17th, Chief Allen reports again, 150,000 men in the rebel Army of the Potomac—a report just as reliable as the first. May 3d, from camp at Yorktown, he states the force to be from 100,000 to 120,000, and bases this information upon reports of persons connected with the Commissary Department at Yorktown.

He finally states to General McClellan that these statements are "under rather than over the truth." The truth is, there were not over 53,000 effective men there. From Camp Lincoln, June 26th, he reports that the forces at that time were over 180,000 men. We know they did not amount to more than 85,000, while their official returns give them but 80,000. Finally, on August 14th, he reports that the rebel army about Richmond contained 200,000 men, and that their losses in the seven days' battles were 40,000 men.* They lost 18,000.†

General McClellan remained behind at Yorktown, to push Franklin and Porter to a point twenty miles beyond Williamsburg, but failed to do so in time to render their flank movement of any decided effect.

Now, it turned out that the battle of Williamsburg was fought without any plan, and General McClellan has been censured for having relied too much upon the discretion and ability of the corps commanders present. His absence from the field has been referred to somewhat in detail by the Committee on the Conduct of the War, and in his testimony before that committee the General stated that he was not informed of the nature of the contest, but distinctly states that he considered it at that period a mere affair with the rear-guard of the enemy. In his official report he very naturally places some blame upon the members of his staff who failed to inform him of the operations in the advance.

In justice to General McClellan we must state that he was exceedingly kind-hearted in his animadversions upon the action of his staff officers. At that time the general staff of the Army of the Potomac did not and could not assist him as a General Commanding should have been assisted. There

---

* See Allen's Report, p. 521. Mil. Repts. War Dept., vol. iv.

† See Taylor: Four Years with General Lee. 1878.

was a good organization of the special staff departments at the army headquarters, but there was not a large personal staff of experienced and talented officers, capable of keeping the General fully informed of the operations of his corps, and of the necessity for his presence when that necessity became obvious. The following is his report concerning the battle of Williamsburg:

> "At an early hour of the morning I had sent two of my aids to observe the operations in front, with instructions to report to me everything of importance that might occur. I received no information from them leading me to suppose that there was anything occurring of more importance than a simple affair of a rear-guard, until about 1 o'clock P.M., when a despatch arrived from one of them that everything was not progressing favorably."

This report of the General has called for these remarks in regard to the formation of his general staff, and we find good cause for this condition of affairs. From the Report of the Committee on the Conduct of the War, we gather, upon reading the testimony of General Richardson, and the character of the questions submitted to him, that there had been at that time a strong adverse feeling in regard to the composition and number of the staff of the General Commanding the Army of the Potomac. It was but natural, therefore, that General McClellan felt that the Government and the public were not ready to understand the necessities of his position in this regard, and that he abstained from requiring the necessary details from the army and appointments at large to his staff in deference to these views. General McClellan's field-work was therefore restricted by this unwillingness on his part to relieve himself from the burden of the details which afterward crowded upon him.

It was probably the duty of the Government to appoint to

the general staff many prominent foreigners who desired to observe our military operations, and, as in the case of the French princes, such officers might at times render brilliant services; but their presence should not have excluded American officers of ability and experience.

Most of his failures were due to these causes. No one seemed to encourage action or to report when or where he could act. He could not be present at all times with his advance, and often no one represented him at this point. He endeavored to do in person that which he should have done through a proper staff. The result was apparent inefficiency on his part and want of unity in the efforts of his corps.

After the evacuation of Yorktown, the main body of the Army of the Potomac had a plain duty to perform, *i.e.,* to overtake the enemy—to engage him—to capture or detain him until his flank should be gained by Franklin's command. The performance of this duty was very naturally left to the next general in order of rank—the commander of the first corps—when General McClellan deemed it to be his duty to remain at Yorktown to push the selected force rapidly to Eltham. But unfortunately the troops could not be pushed rapidly to Eltham, and the result of his labors at this point did not compensate for the loss of his presence at Williamsburg. He could not know it, but at that time it is stated by the rebel General Hood that General Johnston had made up his mind to retreat beyond Richmond, and to detain him anywhere was of the greatest importance.

If General McClellan could have been informed at once of what was occurring at Williamsburg, he would have gone there, and, by his presence and with his knowledge of his own plans, he would have forced the rebels to have abandoned their works at once, or he would have detained them in their lines until he could have succeeded in placing Generals Franklin, Porter, Sedgwick, and Richardson on their flank. At any rate, he would have punished them more severely, knowing that they were forced to fight to save their trains, and also forced to retreat to save their communications with Richmond. Here, by reason of his absence and by reason of the want of knowledge of the position of affairs on the part of his staff officers, he failed in all his plans most signally, and the failure appeared all the greater because he had promised rapid marches and brilliant operations. The rain and the mud were nearly as bad for the rebels as for the United States troops. Another fatal error was made, and an opportunity to inspirit the whole army and the Government was lost on May 5, 1862.

General Johnston reports that at no time was he pressed or uncertain. Two-thirds of the Union army under its senior corps commander could have both "pressed" him and produced "uncertainty." For work of this kind no man save the General Commanding himself was fitted at that time. Johnston actually got away from the Union front and attacked General Franklin's turning or flanking column on the 7th inst., at 10 A.M., and drove a portion of it out of his way, and so passed on.

However, we did derive some benefits from the battle of Williamsburg. Generals Hancock, Kearney, and Hooker then and there gave evidence of their fitness for command on such occasions.

The reasons assigned for not following Johnston more rapidly were the exhaustion of the troops, want of ammunition, the want of rations, the rain, and the mud. The Army of the Potomac was hampered by the necessity for establishing a new base, and the result was that it was not until twelve days after the battle of Williamsburg that it arrived in front of Richmond. Concerning the events following the assumption of the advanced position in front of Richmond, there is little beyond what has been narrated to which we would desire to call attention. An army inexperienced in field operations had been finally brought near to the rebel capital. It was enthusiastic and confident, but it needed an especial training to carry on an offensive campaign. It is therefore impossible for us to agree with General Barnard in regard to the affair of Hanover Court-House, which he calls a useless battle. In point of fact this battle was exactly what the army wanted. If there was to be a junction made with McDowell, it was well to drive General Branch out of the way, even if it was not necessary to do so. But, beyond all this, it was high time for the new army to exhibit some character and determination in its operations; and all successful affairs of this kind, whether on its flanks or in its front, would have been of importance as giving esprit and morale to the forces engaged; and would have assisted in developing the talents and increasing the experience of the generals taking part in them. To the Army of the Potomac, for these reasons, the battle of Hanover Court-House was of great service. The writer made the preliminary reconnoissance with the cavalry, and guided the column of General Porter when he moved to defeat General Branch, and to communicate if possible with General McDowell. He knows the effect upon the troops of our success at that point, and he considers the moral effects of that success to have been of the greatest importance in the subsequent battle of Gaines' Mill.

The story of Fair Oaks and Seven Pines is well known to all. Since the war we have discovered that we could have gone to Richmond. General McClellan was sick, and if he believed his secret service report he was probably glad to have prevented the overwhelming of his left flank by 150,000 rebels under Johnston. As usual, he was grossly and persistently deceived. But there was another case at Gaines' Mill.

At the battle General McClellan found 70,000 of the enemy on the left bank of the Chickahominy, desperately contending to overwhelm Fitz John Porter, who resolutely defended himself for many hours from being driven into the river, or down it, by this overwhelming force. We have narrated exactly what occurred on both banks of the stream. But the writer was present with General Porter on that day, having been ordered to join him, and having left the general headquarters for that purpose. He carried with him to General Porter the distinct impression then prevailing at the headquarters of the army, that he was to hold this large force of the enemy on the left bank of the Chickahominy, in order that General McClellan, with the main army, might break through and take Richmond. At that time it was generally understood that this was the plan of the General Commanding; if it were not so, the criticism that General Porter should have been taken to the right bank of the river before the battle, is in our opinion the correct one. The sacrifice at Gaines' Mill of 7,000 men was warranted, if we were to gain Richmond by making it, and the troops engaged in carrying out this plan, conceiving it to be the wish of the General Commanding, were successful in holding the rebels on the left bank. But General McClellan had made up his mind to move to the James River to a new base before this battle, and he had made every preparation to make this change in the presence of the army defending Richmond. His subsequent movements and orders clearly show that he did not believe that the entrance of the army into Richmond at that time, leaving the major part of the rebel army on the left bank of the Chickahominy, was a proper military movement. In this view of the military position he has already encountered, as he will always encounter, a strong adverse criticism from most military writers. The whole strength of the United States Government would have been instantly turned toward maintaining his army in the rebel capital, and Generals Lee and Jackson would have had a slight chance of success if they presumed to cross the Chickahominy to its right bank for the purpose of regaining Richmond. From this moment until the taking of the army from the Peninsula, everything seems to have been subordinated to the movements necessary to defend the Union lines from the repeated attacks from the rebels, who, after concentrating their forces on the right bank of the Chickahominy, seemed animated by the hope that they would ultimately drive our army from the Peninsula, or carry much of it to Richmond as prisoners.

Chief Allen about this time reports 200,000 men as opposed to the Army of the Potomac. General McClellan found Porter opposed to about 70,000, and supposed 125,000 men were in position between him and Richmond. He thereupon made *one* of the most able flank movements ever made in war. It may be called "retreat" or change of base, as different writers may prefer; the army certainly did not move of its own accord, as in retreat, but it was directed by General McClellan to its final position at Malvern Hill, and there it fought and maintained its reputation. The lessons taught the Army of the Potomac during the past three months were never lost to it. Inexperienced officers and men became veterans, to serve under other commanders in "defending the constitution of the country and the nationality of its people."*

---

* See General McClellan's farewell order.

And now, what saved the Army of the Potomac from further disaster than that consequent upon a forced change of base? It was the perfection of its organization, which was due to the personal affection entertained for General McClellan by the officers and men of his army. As an evidence of the influence this attachment of the army to the General Commanding had upon the authorities at Washington, we quote the following from a letter addressed to the writer by one of the ablest generals of the regular army, who has from the fall of Sumter until to-day enjoyed the respect and confidence of every administration: "General Hitchcock said to me, I presume about the time he visited the Peninsula, 'It is impossible for me now to command that army,' referring, I understood, to its training by McClellan, its known devotion to him, to the fact that its corps commanders and highest officers were almost entirely of his selection, so that the whole army, officers and men, were in a special manner devoted to him, and would thus be with difficulty guided and controlled by a general new to it and to them, and whose military reputation belonged to a long-passed war—that with Mexico."

These officers were correct in their estimate of the influence which this personal affection for its commander had upon the Army of the Potomac. It was so strong that every one naturally shrank from interfering between General McClellan and his men. His own regard for his troops may have at times made him unwilling to sacrifice some for the good of the whole. It is but charitable to consider this feeling on his part to have been one cause of our failure. We must write, however, in regard to facts of history just as the record presents these facts to us. There was failure, and the causes of that failure have been largely hidden from us. We, who belonged to the Army of the Potomac, the grandest army gathered on this continent, at all times true to its commander-in-chief, whoever it might be, hope that he who organized that army will yet deem it wise and proper to give some fuller vindication of the policy he adopted, no matter whom he may strike. As it is, his friends and admirers have to deplore the necessity of writing in general criticism of the results which have been variously attributed to "want of support," "interference," or "inaction."

APPENDIX A.

THE original organization of the Army of the Potomac was of a temporary character, extending no farther than the formation of brigades and divisions, in which subsequent changes were to be made, as their efficiency demanded. The final composition, on April 1, 1862, commencing with the portion which went to the Peninsula, and giving afterward the regiments and batteries left on the Potomac, in Maryland and Virginia, was as follows:*

TROOPS OF THE ARMY OF THE POTOMAC SENT TO THE PENINSULA IN MARCH AND APRIL, 1862.

I.
CAVALRY RESERVE. BRIGADIER-GENERAL P. ST. G. COOKE.

Emory's Brigade,
5th United States Cavalry.
6th " "
6th Pennsylvania "

Blake's Brigade.
1st United States Cavalry.
8th Pennsylvania "
Barker's Squadron Illinois Cavalry.

II.
ARTILLERY RESERVE. COLONEL HENRY J. HUNT.

Graham's Battery	"K" & "G"	1st U. S.,	6	Napoleon guns.
Randol's "	"E"	1st "	6	" "
Carlisle's "	"E"	2d "	6	20-pds. Parrott guns.
Robertson's "		2d "	6	3-inch ordnance guns.
Benson's "	"M"	2d "	6	" " "
Tidball's "	"A"	2d "	6	" " "
Edwards' "	"L" & "M"	3d "	6	10-pds. Parrott "
Gibson's "	"C" & "G"	3d "	6	3-inch ordnance "
Livingston's "	"F" & "K"	3d "	4	10-pds. Parrott "
Howe's "	"G"	4th "	6	Napoleon "
De Russy's "	"K"	4th "	6	" "
Weed's "	"I"	5th "	6	3-inch ordnance "

---

* This Roster is taken from General McClellan's official report, as published by himself.

Smead's Battery	"K"	5th U. S.,	4 Napoleon guns.
Ames' "	"A"	5th "	6 { 4 10-pds. Parrott / 2 Napoleon } guns.
Diederick's "	"A" N. Y. Art. Batt'n,		6 20-pds. Parrott guns.
Voegelie's "	"B" " " "		4 " " "
Knieriem's "	"C" " " "		4 " " "
Grimm's "	"D" " " "		6 32-pds. howitzers.
			100 guns.

III.

VOLUNTEER ENGINEER TROOPS. GENERAL WOODBURY.

15th New York Volunteers.
50th " "

REGULAR ENGINEER TROOPS. CAPTAIN DUANE.

Companies "A," "B," and "C," U. S. Engineers.

ARTILLERY TROOPS WITH SIEGE TRAIN.

1st Connecticut Heavy Artillery. *Col. Tyler.*

INFANTRY RESERVE (REGULAR BRIGADE). GENERAL SYKES.

Nine Companies 2d United States Infantry.
Seven " 3d " "
Ten " 4th " "
Ten " 6th " "
Eight " 10th & 17th " "
Six " 11th " "
Eight " 12th " "
Nine " 14th " "
5th New York Volunteers. *Col. Warren.*

SECOND CORPS. GENERAL SUMNER.

CAVALRY.

8th Illinois Cavalry. *Col. Farnsworth.*
One Squadron 6th New York Cavalry.

RICHARDSON'S DIVISION.

ARTILLERY.

Clark's Battery	"A" & "C"	4th U. S.,	6 Napoleon guns.
Frank's "	"G"	1st N.Y.,	6 10-pds. Parrott guns.
Pettit's "	"B"	1st "	6 " " "
Hogan's "	"A"	2d "	6 " " "

INFANTRY.

Howard's Brigade.	*Meagher's Brigade.*	*French's Brigade.*
5th N. H. Vols.	69th N. Y. Vols.	52d N. Y. Vols.
81st Penn. "	63d " "	57th " "
61st N. Y. "	88th " "	66th " "
64th " "		53d Penn. "

SEDGWICK'S DIVISION.

ARTILLERY.

Kirby's Battery "I" 1st U. S., 6 Napoleon guns.
Tompkins " "A" 1st R. I., 6 { 4 10-pds. Parrott / 2 12-pds. Howitzers } guns.
Bartlett's " "B" 1st " 6 { 4 10-pds. Parrott / 2 12-pds. Howitzers } guns.
Owen's " "G" — —, 6 3-inch ordnance guns.

INFANTRY.

Gorman's Brigade.	*Burns' Brigade.*	*Dana's Brigade.*
2d N. Y. S. M.	69th Penn. Vols.	19th Mass. Vols.
15th Mass. Vols.	71st " "	7th Mich. "
34th N. Y. "	72d " "	42d N. Y. "
1st Minn. "	106th " "	20th Mass. "

NOTE.—*Blenker's division* detached and assigned to the *Mountain Department.*

THIRD CORPS. GENERAL HEINTZELMAN.

CAVALRY.

3d Pennsylvania Cavalry. *Col. Averill.*

PORTER'S DIVISION.

ARTILLERY.

Griffin's Battery "K" 5th U. S., 6 10-pds. Parrot guns.
Weeden's " "C" R. I., — — — —
Martin's " "C" Mass., 6 Napoleon guns.
Allen's " "E" " 6 3-in. ordnance guns.

INFANTRY.

Martindale's Brigade.	*Morell's Brigade.*	*Butterfield's Brigade.*
2d Maine Vols.	14th N. Y. Vols.	17th N. Y. Vols.
18th Mass. "	4th Mich. "	83d Penn. "
22d " "	9th Mass. "	44th N. Y. "
25th N. Y. "	62d Penn. "	Stockton's Michigan.
13th " "		12th N. Y. Vols.
1st Berdan Sharpshooters.		

HOOKER'S DIVISION.

ARTILLERY.

Hall's Battery "H" 1st U. S., 6 { 4 10-pds. Parrott / 2 12-pds. Howitzers } guns.
Smiths " 4th N. Y. Battery, 6 10-pds. Parrott guns.
Bramhall's " 6th " " 6 3-in. ordnance "
Osborn's " "D" 1st N. Y. Art'y, 4 " " "

INFANTRY.

Sickles' Brigade.	*Nagle's Brigade.*	*Col. Starr's Brigade.*
1st Excelsior (N. Y.)	1st Mass. Vols.	5th N. J. Vols.
2d " "	11th " "	6th " "
3d " "	26th Penn. "	7th " "
4th " "	2d N. H. "	8th " "
5th " "		

HAMILTON'S DIVISION.*

ARTILLERY.

Thompson's Battery "G" 2d U. S., 6 Napoleon guns.
Beam's " "B" N. J., 6 { 4 10-pds. Parrott / 2 Napoleon } guns.
Randolph's " "E" R. I., 6 { 4 10-pds. Parrott / 2 Napoleon } "

---

* Afterward Kearny's Division.

INFANTRY.

Jameson's Brigade.	*Birney's Brigade.*	*Berry's Brigade.*
105th Penn. Vols.	38th N. Y. Vols.	2d Mich. Vols.
63d “ “	40th “ “	3d “ “
57th “ “	3d Maine “	5th “ “
87th N. Y. “	4th “ “	37th N. Y. “

FOURTH CORPS. GENERAL KEYES.

CAVALRY.

COUCH'S DIVISION.

ARTILLERY.

McCarty's Battery	“C” 1st Penn.,	4 10 pds. Parrott guns.
Flood's “	“D” 1st “	6 “ “ “
Miller's “	“E” 1st “	4 Napoleon “ “
Brady's “	“H” 1st “	4 10-pds. Parrott “

INFANTRY.

Graham's Brigade.	*Peck's Brigade.*	*Devin's Brigade.**
67th N. Y. Vols (1st L. I.)	98th Penn. Vols.	2d R. I. Vols.
65th “ “ (1st U. S. Chas.)	102d “ “	7th Mass. “
23d Penn. “	93d “ “	10th “ “
31st “ “	62d N. Y. “	36th N. Y. “
61st “ “	65th “ “	

SMITH'S DIVISION.

ARTILLERY.

Ayres' Battery	“F” 5th U. S.,	6 { 4 10-pds. Parrott 2 Napoleon }	guns.
Mott's “	3d N. Y. Battery,	6 { 4 10-pds. Parrott 2 Napoleon }	“
Wheeler's “	“E” 1st N Y.,	4 3 in. ordnance	“
Kennedy's “	1st N. Y. Battery,	6 “ “	“

INFANTRY.

Hancock's Brigade.	*Brooks' Brigade.*	*Davidson's Brigade.*
5th Wis. Vols.	2d Vermont Vols.	33d N. Y. Vols.
49th Penn. “	3d “ “	77th “ “
43d N. Y. “	4th “ “	49th “ “
6th Maine “	5th “ “	7th Maine “
	6th “ “	

CASEY'S DIVISION.

ARTILLERY.

Regan's Battery	7th N. Y. Battery,	6 3-in. ordnance guns.
Fitch's “	8th “ “	6 “ “ “
Bates' “	“A” 1st N. Y. Art'y,	6 Napoleon “
Spratt's “	“H” 1st “ “	4 3-in. ordnance “

INFANTRY.

Keim's Brigade.	*Palmer's Brigade.*	*Naglee's Brigade.*
85th Penn. Vols.	85th N. Y. Vols.	104th Penn. Vols.
101st “ “	98th “ “	52d “ “
103d “ “	92d “ “	56th N. Y. “
96th N. Y. “	81st “ “	100th “ “
	93d “ “	11th Maine “

* Afterward Palmer's.

V.

PROVOST GUARD.

2d U. S. Cavalry.
Battalion 8th and 17th U. S. Infantry.

AT GENERAL HEADQUARTERS.

2 Cos. 4th U. S. Cavalry. 1 Co. Oneida Cav. (N. Y. Vols.).
1 Co. Sturgis Rifles (Ill. Vols.).

The following troops of the Army of the Potomac were left behind, or detached, on and in front of the Potomac for the defense of that line, April 1, 1862. Franklin's and McCall's divisions at subsequent and different dates joined the active portion of the army on the Peninsula. Two brigades of Shields' division joined at Harrison's Landing.

FIRST CORPS. GENERAL McDOWELL.

CAVALRY.

1st New York Cavalry.
2d " "
4th New York Cavalry.
1st Pennsylvania "

SHARPSHOOTERS.

2d Regiment Berdan's Sharpshooters.

FRANKLIN'S DIVISION.

ARTILLERY.

Platt's Battery	"D" 2d U. S.,	6 Napoleon guns.	
Porter's "	"A" Mass.,	6 { 4-10 pds. Parrott / 2 12-pds. Howitzers }	guns.
Hexamer's "	"A" N. J.,	6 { 4 10-pds. Parrott / 2 12-pds. Howitzers }	"
Wilson's "	"F" 1st N.Y. Art'y,	4 3-in. ordnance	"

INFANTRY.

Kearney's *Brigade.*	*Slocum's Brigade.*	*Newton's Brigade.*
1st N. J. Vols.	16th N. Y. Vols.	18th N. Y. Vols.
2d " "	27th " "	31st " "
3d " "	5th Maine "	32d " "
4th " "	96th Penn. "	95th Penn. "

McCALL'S DIVISION.

ARTILLERY.

Seymour's Battery	"C"	5th U. S.,	6	Napoleon guns.
Easton's "	"A"	1st Penn.,	4	" "
Cooper's "	"B"	1st "	6	10-pds. Parrott guns.
Kern's "	"C"	1st "	6	{ 2 10-pds. Parrott / 4 12-pds. Howitzers } guns.

INFANTRY.

Reynolds' Brigade.	*Meade's Brigade*	*Ord's Brigade.*
1st Penn. Res. Reg't.	3d Penn. Res. Reg't.	6th Penn. Res. Reg't.
2d " " "	4th " " "	9th " " "
5th " " "	7th " " "	10th " " "
8th " " "	11th " " "	12th " " "
	1 Penn. Reserve Rifles.	

KING'S DIVISION.

ARTILLERY.

Gibbon's Battery	"B" 4th U. S.,	6 Napoleon guns.
Monroe's "	"D" 1st R. I.,	6 10-pds. Parrott guns.
Gerrish's "	"A" N. H.,	6 Napoleon. "
Durrell's "	Penn.	6 10-pds. Parrott "

INFANTRY.

—Brigade.	*Patrick's Brigade.*	*Augur's Brigade.*
2d Wis. Vols.	20th N. Y. S. M.	14th N. Y. S. M.
6th " "	21st " Vols.	22d " Vols.
7th " "	23d " "	24th " "
19th Ind. "	25th " "	30th " "

FIFTH CORPS. GENERAL BANKS.

CAVALRY.

1st Maine Cavalry.	5th New York Cavalry.
1st Vermont "	8th " "
1st Michigan "	Keyes' Battalion Penn. Cavalry.
1st R. I. "	18 Cos. Maryland "
	1 Squadron Virginia "

Unattached.

28th Penn. Vols. 4th Reg't Potomac Home Guard (Maryland Vols.).

WILLIAMS' DIVISION.

ARTILLERY.

Best's Battery	"F" 4th U. S.,	6 Napoleon guns.
Hampton's "	Maryland,	4 10-pds. Parrott guns.
Thompson's "	"	4 " " "
Mathews' "	"F" Penn.	6 3-in. ordnance "
——— "	"M" 1st N. Y.	6 10-pds. Parrott "
Knapp's "	Penn.	6 " " "
McMahon's "	N. Y.	6 3-in. ordnance "

INFANTRY.

Abercrombie's Brigade.	*—Brigade.*	*—Brigade.*
12th Mass. Vols.	9th N. Y. S. M.	28th N. Y. Vols.
2d " "	29th Penn. Vols.	5th Conn. "
16th Ind. "	27th Ind. "	46th Penn. "
1st Potomac Home Brigade (Md. Vols.).	3d Wis. "	1st Maryland "
1 Co. Zouaves d'Afrique (Penn. Vols.).		12th Ind. "
		13th Mass. "

SHIELDS' DIVISION.

Artillery.

Clark's	Battery	"E" 4th U. S.,	6 10-pds. Parrott guns.
Jenks'	"	" A " 1st Va.,	6 { 4 10-pds. Parrott / 2 6-pds. } guns.
Davy's	"	"B" 1st "	2 10-pds Parrott guns.
Huntington's	"	"A" 1st Ohio,	6 13-pds. James "
Robinson's	"	" L " 1st "	6 { 2 12-pds. Howitzers / 4 6-pds. } guns.
		4th Ohio Inf'y,	1 6-pds. gun.

Infantry.

—Brigade.	*—Brigade.*	*—Brigade.*
14th Ind. Vols.	5th Ohio Vols.	7th Ohio Vols.
4th Ohio "	62d " "	29th " "
8th " "	66th " "	7th " "
7th Va. "	13th Ind. "	1st Va. "
67th Ohio "	39th Ill. "	11th Penn "
84th Penn. "		Andrew Sharpshooters.

GENERAL WADSWORTH'S COMMAND.

Cavalry.

1st New Jersey Cavalry, at Alexandria.
4th Pennsylvania " east of the capital.

Artillery and Infantry.

10th New Jersey Vols.	Bladensburg Road.
104th N. Y. Vols.	Kalorama Heights.
1st Wis. Heavy Art'y.	Fort "Cass," Va.
3 Batteries N. Y. "	Forts "Ethan Allen" and "Marcy."
Depot of N. Y. Light Art'y.	Camp "Barry."
2d D. C. Vols.	Washington City.
26th Penn. "	G St. Wharf.
26th N. Y. "	Fort "Lyon."
95th " "	Camp "Thomas."
94th " "	Alexandria.
88th Penn. " (Detachment).	"
91st " "	Franklin Square Barracks.
4th N. Y. Art'y.	Forts "Carroll" and "Greble."
112th Penn. Vols.	Fort "Saratoga."
76th N.Y. "	" "Massachusetts."
59th " "	" "Pennsylvania."
88th Penn " (Detachment).	" "Good Hope."
99th " "	" "Mahan."
2d N. Y. Light Art'y.	Forts "Ward," "Worth," and "Blenker."
107th Penn Vols.	Kendall Green.
54th " "	" "
Dickerson's Light Art'y.	East of the capital.
86th N. Y. Vols.	" " "
98th Penn. " (Detachment).	" " "
14th Mass. " (Heavy Art'y).	{ Forts "Albany," "Tellinghast," "Richardson," "Runyon," "Jackson," "Barnard," "Craig," "Scott."
56th Penn. "	
4th U. S. Art'y (Detachment).	{ Fort "Washington."
37th N. Y. Vols. (Detachment).	" "
97th " "	Fort "Corcoran."
101st " "	
12th Va. "	
91st N. Y. "	

IN CAMP NEAR WASHINGTON.

6th New York Cavalry, Dismounted.
10th " " "
Swaim's " " "
2d Pennsylvania " "

(These troops, 3,359 men, were ordered to report to Colonel Miles, commanding Railroad Guard, to relieve 3,306 older troops, ordered to be sent to Manassas to report to General Abercrombie.)

GENERAL DIX'S COMMAND. (BALTIMORE.)

CAVALRY.

1st Maryland Cavalry. Detachment of Cav. Purnell Legion.

ARTILLERY.

Battery "I" 2d U. S. Artillery.
" — Maryland Artillery.
" "L" 1st New York Artillery.
2 Independent Batteries, Pennsylvania Artillery.

INFANTRY.

3d New York Volunteers.
4th " "
11th Pennsylvania" "
87th " "
111th " "
21st Massachusetts" (Detachment).
2d Delaware "
2d Maryland "
1st Eastern Shore Home Guards (Maryland Volunteers).
2d " " " " " "
Purnell Legion (Maryland Volunteers).
2 Battalions ———.

In this mere outline of the formation of the Army of the Potomac, it is impossible to treat of the eminent services of the prominent members of the general staff in detail. The erection of a line of forts covering a large city like Washington,—a line thirty-three miles in length, was the work of able engineers under General Barnard. He well represented the corps of United States Engineers, of which the country has always been proud. Skill and diligent labor were necessary, and the Commanding General gives full credit to all engaged in the work, in his final report. General Barton S. Alexander, General D. P. Woodbury, and Captain J. C. Duane organized and equipped the engineer troops, comprising the United States Engineers, the Fifteenth New York Volunteers, and the Fiftieth New York Volunteers, the latter well adapted for this service, containing, as they did, many sailors and mechanics. Captain Duane prepared the engineer and bridge train, afterward so necessary to the movements of our army. By General William F. Barry, Chief of Artillery, eighty-one batteries were organized and equipped in a few months,—thirty regular and sixty-two volunteers, if we include the nine present after Bull Run. General Stoneman, in spite of all obstacles, rendered a praiseworthy service in giving to the army its first real cavalry organization.

APPENDIX B.

CONFEDERATE NAMES OF THE SKIRMISHES AND BATTLES AROUND RICHMOND.

EVENTS.

May 31st, Battle of Seven Pines, Va.
June 1st, Battle of Fair Oaks, Va.
June 13th to 15th, Pamunkey Expedition, Va.
June 15th, Skirmish at Seven Pines, Va.
June 18th, Skirmish at Nine Mile Road, Va.
June 20th, Affair at Gill's Bluff, James River, Va.
June 25th, Battle of King's Schoolhouse (French Field, Oak Grove, or the Orchard), Va.
June 25th, 26th, Artillery Engagement on Garnett's Farm, Va.
June 26th, Engagement at Point of Rocks, Appomattox River, Va.
June 26th, Skirmish at Atlee's Station, Va.
June 26th, 27th, Skirmishes at Hundley's Corner, Va.
June 26th, 27th, Battle of Mechnnicsville or Ellison's Mills, Va.
June 27th, Battle of Cold Harbor, or Gaines' Farm, Va.
June 27th, Engagement at Garnett's Hill, Va.
June 28th, Affair near Garnett's House, Va.
June 29th, Battle of Savage Station, Va.
June 29th, Battle of Garnett's Farm, Va.
June 30th, Battle of Frazier's Farm, Va.
June 30th, Battle of White Oak Swamp, Va.
June 30th, Affair at Willis Church, near Malvern Hill, Va.
June 30th, Engagement at Turkey Bridge, or Malvern Cliff, Va.
July 1st, Battle of Malvern Hill, or Crew's Farm, Va.
July 2d, Affair near Haxall's Landing, Va.
July 4th, Skirmish at Westover, Va.

ORGANIZATION OF THE ARMY OF NORTHERN VIRGINIA DURING ENGAGEMENTS AROUND RICHMOND, VA.

JACKSON'S CORPS.

MAJOR-GENERAL T. J. JACKSON, COMMANDING.

FIRST DIVISION.

BRIGADIER-GENERAL W. H. C. WHITING.

First Brigade.

Brig.-Gen. J. B. HOOD.
18th Georgia.
1st Texas.
4th Texas.
5th Texas.
Hampton Legion.

Third Brigade.

(1) Brig.-Gen. WHITING,
(2) Col. LAW, Com'd'g.
2d Mississippi.
11th Mississippi.
4th Alabama.
6th North Carolina.
Staunton Artillery.

*Fourth Brigade.**

Brig.-Gen. A. R. LAWTON.
Reilly's Battery.
Balthis' Battery.

SECOND DIVISION.

MAJOR-GENERAL T. J. JACKSON.

First Brigade.

Brig.-Gen. C. S. WINDER.
2d Virginia.
4th "
5th "
27th "
33d "
Irish Battalion (Capt. Lee).
Rockbridge Artillery.
Carpenter's Battery.

Second Brigade.

(1) —— JONES.
(2) Col. CUNNINGHAM, Com'd'g
21st Virginia.
42d "
48th "
1st Virginia Battalion.
Hampden Artillery.
Jackson's "

Third Brigade.

(1) Col. J. V. FULBERSON,
(2) Col. E. T. H. WARREN, Com'd'g.
10th Virginia.
23d "
37th "
Wooding's Battery.
Danville Artillery.

Fourth Brigade.

Brig. Geo. A. R. LAWTON.
13th Georgia
26th "
31st "
38th "
60th " or 4th Battalion.
61st "

THIRD DIVISION.

MAJOR-GENERAL R. S. EWELL.

Fourth Brigade.

(1) Brig.-Gen. A. ELZEY, and
(2) Brig.-Gen. J. A. EARLY, Com'd'g.
13th Virginia.
25th "
31st "
44th "
52d "
58th "
12th Georgia.

Seventh Brigade.

Brig.-Gen'l I. R. TRIMBLE.
15th Alabama.
21st Georgia.
16th Mississippi.
21st North Carolina.
Wharton's Battalion.

---

* Transferred to Jackson's Division.

Eighth Brigade.

(1) Col. Seymour, and
(2) Col. L. A. Stafford, Com'd'g.
6th Louisiana.
7th "
8th "
9th "

Maryland Line.

Col. B. T. Johnbon.
Brockenbrough's Battery.
Courtenay's "
Carrington's "
Munford's Cavalry.

MAJOR-GENERAL D. H. HILL'S DIVISION.*

First Brigade.

Brig.-Gen. R. E. Rodes.
3d Alabama.
5th "
6th "
12th "
26th "
Carter's Battery.

Second Brigade.

Brig.-Gen. G. B. Anderson.
2d North Carolina.
4th " "
14th " "
30th " "
Hardaway's Battery.

Third Brigade.

Brig.-Gen. S. Garland.
5th North Carolina.
12th " "
13th " "
20th " "
23d " "
Bondurant's Battery.

Fourth Brigade.

Col. A. H. Colquitt.
6th Georgia.
23d "
27th "
28th "

Fifth Brigade.

Brig.-Gen. R. S. Ripley.
1st North Carolina.
3d " "
44th Georgia.
48th "
Rhett's Battery.
Jones' Artillery.
Nelson's Artillery.

MAJOR-GENERAL J. B. MAGRUDER'S COMMAND.

FIRST DIVISION.

BRIGADIER-GENERAL D. R. JONES.

First Brigade.

Brig.-Gen. R. Toombs.
2d Georgia.
15th "
17th "
20th "

Third Brigade.

Col. G. T. Anderson.
1st Georgia (Regulars).
7th "
8th "
9th "
11th "
Garnett's Battery.
Brown's "
Lane's "

McLAWS' DIVISION.

MAJOR-GENERAL L. McLAWS.

First Brigade.

Brig.-Gen. P. J. Semmes.
10th Georgia.
53d "
15th Virginia.
32d "

Fourth Brigade.

Brig.-Gen. J. B. Kershaw.
2d South Carolina
3d " "
7th " "
8th " "
Alexander's Artillery.

---

* This was not a part of Jackson's corps, but co-operated with it.

MAJOR-GENERAL J. B. MAGRUDER'S DIVISION.

Second Brigade.

Brig.-Gen. HOWELL COBB.
2d Louisiana.
15th North Carolina.
16th Georgia.
24th “
Cobb's Georgia Legion.

Third Brigade.

Col. WM. BARKSDALE.
13th Mississippi.
17th “
18th “
21st “

Colonel S. D. LEE, Chief of Artillery (temporarily).

LONGSTREET'S DIVISION.*

NOTE.—At battles of Seven Pines and Fair Oaks, Va., Longstreet commanded the right wing and G. W. Smith the left wing, subsequent to which Smith's command appears to have been scattered among others.

First Brigade.

Brig. Gen. J. L. KEMPER.
1st Virginia.
7th “
11th “
17th “
24th “
Rogers' Battery.

Second Brigade.

Brig.-Gen. R. H. ANDERSON.
2d South Carolina.
4th “ “
5th “ “
6th “ “
Palmetto Sharpshooters.

Third Brigade.

(1) Brig.-Gen. PICKETT,
(2) Col. J. B. STRANGE, Commanding.
8th Virginia.
18th “
19th “
28th “
56th “

Fourth Brigade.

Brig.-Gen. C. M. WILCOX.
8th Alabama.
9th “
10th “
11th “
Thomas' Artillery (Capt. Anderson).

Fifth Brigade.

Brig.-Gen. R. A. PRYOR.
3d Virginia.
2d Florida.
14th Alabama.
14th Louisiana.
Louisiana Zouaves.

Sixth Brigade.

Brig.-Gen. W. G. FETHERSTON.
12th Mississippi.
19th “
2d Mississippi Battalion.

NOTE.—First Company Washington Artillery temporarily attached to S. D. Lee's Artillery in engagements of July 5th, 6th, 7th, and 8th—Col. S. D. Lee, commanding artillery.

HUGER'S DIVISION.†

MAJOR-GENERAL B. HUGER, COMMANDING.

Second Brigade.‡

Brig.-Gen. R. RANSOM, Jr.
19th North Carolina.
24th
25th “ “
26th “ “
35th “ “
48th “ “
49th “ “

Second Brigade.

Brig.-Gen. WM. MAHONE.
6th Virginia.
12th “
16th “
41st “
49th “
Grimes' Battery.

Third Brigade.

Brig.-Gen. A. R. WRIGHT.
1st Louisiana.
3d Georgia.
4th “
22d “
44th Alabama.
Huger's Battery.

Fourth Brigade.

Brig.-Gen. L. A. ARMISTEAD.
9th Virginia.
14th “
38th “
53d
57th “
5th “ Battalion.
Turner's Battery.
Stribling's Battery.

---

* Called right wing at Seven Pines.
† This corresponds with return on file in Archive Office.
‡ Belongs to Department of North Carolina, temporarily attached to this Division.

WALKER'S BRIGADE.

Attached June 26th; detached June 27th. (See Holmes' command.)

LIGHT DIVISION.

MAJOR-GENERAL A. P. HILL, COMMANDING.

First Brigade.

Brig.-Gen. CHAS. W. FIELD.
40th Virginia.
47th "
55th "
60th "
Pegram's Battery.

Second Brigade.

Brig.-Gen. M. GREGG.
1st South Carolina.
12th " "
13th " "
14th " "
1st " " Rifles.
Pee Dee Artillery (McIntosh's).

Third Brigade.

Brig.-Gen. J. R. ANDERSON.
14th Georgia.
35th "
45th "
3d Louisiana Battalion.
Davidson's Battery.
Letcher Art'y (Greenlee).

Fourth Brigade.

Brig.-Gen. L. O. B. BRANCH.
7th North Carolina.
18th " "
28th " "
33d " "
37th " "
Johnson's Battery.

Fifth Brigade.

Brig.-Gen. J. J. ARCHER.
1st Tennessee.
7th "
14th "
2d Arkansas.
19th Georgia.
5th Alabama Battalion.

Sixth Brigade.

Brig.-Gen. W. D. PENDER.
16th North Carolina.
22d " "
34th " "
38th " "
2d Arkansas Battalion.
Andrews' Battery.
2d Virginia Artillery.
Crenshaw's Battery.
Masters' Battery.*
—Virginia Battalion.

DEPARTMENT OF NORTH CAROLINA.

MAJOR-GENERAL T. H. HOLMES, COMMANDING.

Ransom's Brigade.

Temporarily attached to Huger's Division. (See Huger's Division.)

Third Brigade.

Brig.-Gen. J. DANIEL.
43d North Carolina.
45th " "
50th " "
Brem's Battery.
Graham's Battery.
Burrough's Cavalry Battalion.

Fourth Brigade.

(1) Col. J. A. WALKER,
(2) Col. MANNING, Com'd'g.
30th Virginia.
3d Arkansas.
27th North Carolina.
46th " "
48th* " "
57th Virginia.†
2d Georgia Battalion.
French's Battery.
Branch's Battery.
Goodwin's Cavalry.

WISE'S COMMAND.‡

BRIGADIER-GENERAL H. A. WISE, COMMANDING.

26th Virginia.
46th Virginia.
10th Virginia Cavalry.§
Andrews' Battery.
Rive's Battery.

---

* Temporarily serving with the reserve artillery during this campaign.

† While this brigade was serving with General Huger the 48th North Carolina was substituted for the 57th Virginia.

‡ This corresponds with return on file in Archive Office.

§ Temporarily detached and serving with Stuart.

RESERVE ARTILLERY.

COLONEL JAMES DESHLER, CHIEF OF ARTILLERY.

BRIGADIER-GENERAL W. L. PENDLETON, COMMANDING.

Second Battalion.

Major RICHARDSON.
Ancell's and Milledge's Batteries.
Woolfolk's Battery.
Davidson's and Masters'* Batteries (temporarily).

Sumter Battalion.

Lieut.-Col. CUTTS.
Lane's Battery.
Ross' "
Price's "
Blackshear's Battery.

Third Battalion.

Major Wm. NELSON.
Huckstep's Battery.
Kirkpatrick's "
R. C. M. Page's Battery.

Jones' Battalion.†

Major H. P. JONES.
Clark's Battery.
Peyton's "
Rhett's "

FIRST REGIMENT.

COLONEL J. T. BROWN.

Virginia Artillery.
3d Howitzers (Smith's).
Richmond Fayette Artillery. (Lieut. Clopton's).
Williamsburg Artillery (Captain Coke's).

CAVALRY CORPS.

HAMPTON'S BRIGADE.

1st North Carolina, Baker's.
10th Virginia, Magruder (belonged to Wise's command).
Georgia Legion, Young.
Jeff. Davis Legion (Cavalry) and 4th Virginia, under Martin.
1st Virginia, Fitz Lee.
3d " Goode.
5th " Rosser.
Cobb's Georgia Legion.

NOTE.—From Confederate Military Reports, vol. iv., War Department, Washington, D. C.

---

* Masters' Battery belonged to A. P. Hill's Division.

† Temporarily attached to D. H. Hill's Division.

INDEX.

NOTE.—*Regiments, batteries, etc., are indexed under the names of their States, excepting batteries called by their captain's or by some other special name. These are indexed under* BATTERIES. *Regular troops under* UNITED STATES ARMY.

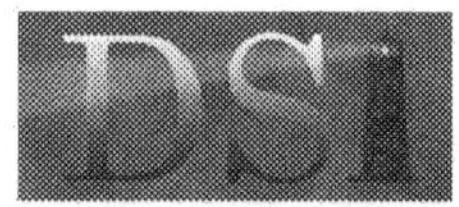

Digital Scanning, Inc.
Scituate, MA 02066
toll free:888-349-4443

www.digitalscanning.com
www.PDFLibrary.com

www.ingramcontent.com/pod-product-compliance
Lightning Source LLC
LaVergne TN
LVHW091046080826
845145LV00002B/647

* 9 7 8 1 5 8 2 1 8 5 2 9 3 *